University of Ulster
LRC, JORDANS

STANDARD LOAN
Return or renew by the date below
Fines will apply to items returned late
If requested, items MUST be returned within 7 days

0 6 MAY 2011		

**Renew items by telephone or online,
24 hours a day, 7 days a week:**
Tel: 028-90368530
http://library.ulster.ac.uk/renew

1323U0000/646/9/2009

©British Association of Social Workers, 1998

All rights reserved. No part of this publication may be reproduced, stored in a retrieval system, or transmitted, in any form or by any means, electronic, mechanical, photo-copying, recording or otherwise, without the prior permission of Venture Press

Published by
VENTURE PRESS
16 Kent Street
Birmingham
B5 6RD

British Library Cataloguing-in-Publication Data
A catalogue record for this book is available from the British Library

ISBN 1-861780-30-3   (paperback)

Cover design by:
Western Arts
194 Goswell Road
London
EC1V 7DT

Printed in Great Britain

Contents

	Page
Preface	v
Chapter 1 Care Management	1
Chapter 2 Care Planning	21
Chapter 3 Yvonne — *Paul Sutton*	41
Chapter 4 Max — *Annie Hawkes*	47
Chapter 5 Mandy — *Althea Brandon*	57
Chapter 6 Kirsty — *Kirsty White*	67
Chapter 7 Joan — *Lana Morris*	73
Chapter 8 Kavin — *Graham Smith*	85
Chapter 9 Mary — *Kate Atherton*	93
Chapter 10 Debbie — *Debbie Tallis*	101
Chapter 11 My Daughter Clare — *Jan Thurlow*	109
Chapter 12 Visions?	113

100454698
362.4
SPE

Preface

This short book concentrates on that key process in care management – care planning. We have used a quotation from the great nineteenth-century, Quaker prison reformer Elizabeth Fry as the title. It summarises that combination of listening and advocacy which all good care planning requires.

We have tried to set the care planning process within the whole context of the needs of people with disabilities for more-individuated systems. For an increasing number that will mean moving towards a direct payment system and outside the existing services. More and more people with disabilities will want their own money to enhance their power and control, as well as to purchase the supports they want – to 'hire and fire'. Increasingly they will find these supports outside the dominant and traditional day and residential services which offer a rather institutional mix.

Care planning will demand a difficult combination of *yin* and *yang* from the professional. It will need the yin of listening and facilitating mixed with the yang of providing structure and form. We have spelt out some of those meanings.

The first two chapters concentrate on the direction of existing policies in community care in relation to care management. They describe the four magnets approach. Then follow a succession of chapters containing individual care plans, communicating some difficulties in their construction. Chapter 9 was originally published in our (Kate Atherton, Althea and David Brandon) 'Care Planning Handbook'. Chapter 11 originally appeared in our 'Money for Change?' Two chapters by Debbie Tallis and Kirsty White record their direct experiences of services and attempts to suggest improved ways of care planning. The last chapter – Visions? – focuses on the existing problems, particularly the structural, and suggests some ideas for the future.

Our thanks to our respective families and to our colleagues and students at the Anglia social work school, in particular to Althea Brandon, Rea Maglajlic and Lana Morris of SHIELD. The book is edited and written by practitioners who have mixed feelings about the whole care management movement. We are moved from depression, seeing how some people experience an awful process, to elation – on seeing genuine empowerment, all too infrequently.

David Brandon
Annie Hawkes
Anglia Polytechnic University
Cambridge

Chapter 1
Care Management

Origins

The beginnings of managing care go back thousands probably even millions of years. Historically, humans planned care for their dependants – children and the elderly, those who could not hunt or gather for themselves.

The parable of the Good Samaritan in the New Testament contains undertones of care management for the Jew who was robbed and injured on the road to Jericho as one might expect from St Luke, the physician. Christ is using this parable as a response to the question: *'Who is my neighbour?'*

St Luke 10 verse 25

A man was on his way from Jerusalem down to Jericho when he fell in with robbers, who stripped him, beat him, and went off leaving him half-dead.

The man was mugged and injured and probably unable to fend for himself, even unconscious. Several people passed by. They were too busy, didn't see him as eligible, didn't want to get involved, or feared for their own well-being lest the muggers return.

But a Samaritan who was making a journey came upon him, and when he saw him was moved to pity. He went up and bandaged his wounds, bathing them with oil and wine.

So this 'care manager' from Samaria, whose nation generally had poor relations with Jews, made an assessment, did some basic first aid, devised a rudimentary care plan. This involved three people – the Jew, himself, and the innkeeper and not a single form!

He lifted him up on to his own beast, brought him to an inn, and looked after him there. Next day he produced two silver pieces and gave them to the innkeeper and said, 'Look after him; and if you spend any more, I will repay you on my way back.'

Nature of the Samaritan's care plan
- first aid through bathing the wounds with oil and wine and then bandaging
- putting him on his own beast
- transport to an inn

- to use direct funding, his own money, so that the Jew could be nursed back to full health
- to finance a key worker – the innkeeper
- to make future arrangements for when the money might run out
- to monitor and evaluate the care plan on his way back from Jericho – to see whether it had been successful, if the Jew had recovered his full health, regained independence.

Rather more recently, Thomas Chalmers, a Glasgow minister, probably the very first social worker, also developed a form of care management. He was concerned about the mis-spending of charitable resources and organised a system of parish visitors to accurately disburse funds raised by the church for those in 'genuine poverty' in 1819. His visitors investigated the conditions of claimants and planned the use of the moneys given. (Brandon and Atherton 1997 pp 4-5)

The Charity Organisation Society founded in London in 1869 built on this pioneering work, recruiting hundreds of volunteers. Amongst their tasks was to 'visit those who have been helped, and to exercise a personal influence over them, so as to ensure that the aid given may be really beneficial. To take charge of individual cases, seeing that the relief required for them, sometimes for a long period, is procured and carefully administered. . . .' (Brandon and Atherton 1997 pp 6-7)

These attempts to help and organise had a shadow side from the earliest beginnings. 'In the first place the applicant for relief is subjected to an examination so close and searching, so absolutely inquisitorial, that no man who could possibly escape from it would submit to it.' (Richmond 1917 p 28, footnote) Care planning was intended to be worse than the Dickensian workhouse!

A Royal Commission report early in the twentieth century expressed the competing pressures with a contemporary ring. 'No country, however rich can permanently hold its own in the race of international competition, if hampered by an increasing load of this dead weight; or can successfully perform the role of sovereignty beyond overseas, if a portion of its own folk at home are sinking below the civilisation and aspirations of its subject races abroad. . . . Great Britain is the home of the voluntary effort, and its triumphs and successes constitute in themselves much of the history of the country. But voluntary effort when attacking a common and ubiquitous evil must be disciplined and led.' (Poor Law Commission 1909)

The idea of care management was also developed in the United States. Weil (1985) traced the roots back to 1863 when Massachusetts established the first Board of Charities co-ordinating the diverse public and voluntary services. By the early 1900s, some settlement houses had developed a rudimentary case co-ordination system. They listed family needs on index cards so that fresh immigrants could be connected with the necessary services and advocated for improved service development.

Case management evolved in the USA to co-ordinate the services provided by numerous health and welfare organisations and developed from an awareness that people got lost in the many labyrinths, often resulting in homelessness. The historical desire to achieve cost effectiveness and the influential consumer and empowerment ideals of the 1960s were also factors.

The modern concept of care management has been in use since the early 1970s and was partly a response for the rapid expansion and increasing complexity of social services, including the growth of multidisciplinary teamwork. For example, the development of psychiatric community care meant large numbers of longstay patients leaving the longstay mental hospitals in both the United States and the United Kingdom. There was a need for more individualised approaches. The United States President's Commission concluded: 'Strategies focused solely on organizations are not enough. A human link is required. A case manager can provide this link and assist in assuring continuity of care and a co-ordinated program of services.' (President's Commission 1978.)

Rapid deinstitutionalisation became a major spur towards new systems. (Rothman 1991). In 1985 the House of Commons Social Services Committee advocated clearly defined care plans and the resources for their implementation for everyone leaving psychiatric hospital. (House of Commons SSC 1984-5)

Griffiths
The report on community care policy by Sir Roy Griffiths (Griffiths 1988) followed by the government White Paper 'Caring for People' (1989) helped those early care management ideas to flourish. The report arose largely out of concerns about rapidly escalating costs especially in the field of services for the elderly, where the financial structures forced expenditure on institution-alised rather than domiciliary solutions.

In 1971-2 social services departments in England and Wales spent £2 billion at present prices (early 1997). By 1996-7 a fourfold increase – £8.4 billion – is expected. In addition, social security expenditure supporting the elderly and other vulnerable people in residential and nursing homes which is being progressively transferred to social services is about £1.75 billion. (DOH 1997 p 2.) The government's Personal Social Services Research Unit commented: 'This increase can only partly be explained by increased labour prices and increased client needs resulting from implementation of community care ... there seems to be a prima facie case that efficiency reduced during the 1980s.' (DOH 1997 p 36)

Central concerns about excessive expenditure were channelled into a drive to enforce the application of big business ideas. Hutton called this state abdication: '... it is the direct consequence of the explosion of home-ownership and the private provision for old age, with the state progressively abdicating its responsibilities in the name of "choice" and "self-reliance".' (Hutton 1995 p 305.) People were expected to stand on their own two feet even though they had none and this cost cutting was justified on moral grounds.

Griffiths was a crucial element in this abdication. It contained an overview of community care policy, recommending that local authority social service departments act as designers, organisers, and purchasers of community care services for all client groups rather than as direct providers. They should develop local plans based on an assessment of community care needs. It also recommended that social services take responsibility for assessing individual needs and arranging purchase of the required services. Local authorities would no longer be primary service providers, this function being taken over by the independent sector. This separation of so-called *purchaser/provider functions* has been extremely influential and inherently destructive of the vital co-operative elements.

Griffiths suggested that care management become one cornerstone of the new community care. It was intended as the core of a package of reforms embedded in free market principles/consumerist ideology, firmly located on the purchaser side of the purchaser/provider divide. Pilot projects were introduced in the 1980s, initially in Kent. These were highly influential and care management became a favourite mechanism of the Department of Health, seen as effective in both addressing need and prioritising resources.

The drive towards the so-called free market, to develop caring as another commodity, was accompanied by the gradual development of shared values centred upon concepts of social inclusion which pushed in radically different directions. This pushed for citizenship rights for those with disabilities; for independence and self-determination; a respect for privacy; an understanding of dignity and individuality; maximising choices; providing services that promoted the individual's aspirations and abilities. (SSI 1991)

These declared values and aspirations linked closely with the spread of 'normalisation' usually understood as 'the principle by which people with a disability have the right to lead a valued ordinary life, based on the belief in their equality as human beings and citizens'. (Ramon 1991) It 'starts from the premise that a major handicap of disabled people is their devaluation in society, and it seeks to remedy this by enabling disabled people, as far as possible, to have experiences that are generally valued in society'. (Wolfensberger 1972)

There was a movement away from the medical model towards social disability. This was fundamentally critical of the medicalisation and individualising of disability, often called the 'personal tragedy' theory. The social disability model stressed people with disabilities playing a full part in society, not simply adapting to structures created by non-disabled people.

'The social model of disability took as its starting point that serious illness and physical or intellectual impairment exist but only become disabling because of the rejecting and oppressive response to such impairments by the non-disabled world. Advocates of the social model (largely disabled people and their allies) argue that the answer to the problem of disability lies in the restructuring of societal attitudes and the physical environment.' (Hall 1997 pp 86-7)

Oliver changes the words of Steve Biko, the murdered South African activist, about black people to express this more fully. 'If by integration you understand a breakthrough into able bodied society by disabled people, an assimilation and acceptance of disabled people into an already established set of norms and code of behaviour set up by the able-bodied, then **YES** I am against it. . . . If on the other hand by integration you mean there shall be participation by all members of a society, catering for the full expression of the self in a freely changing society as determined by people, then I am with you.' (Oliver 1996 p 92)

Community Care Act

The key piece of legislation, the NHS and Community Care Act of 1990, influenced by market economics and to a lesser extent principles of inclusion, required local authorities to re-examine the provision of adult services. In particular, authorities had to establish systems for the assessment of people's social care needs along with the relevant planning and services.

Care management was firmly installed as the preferred means by which community care services could become effective and efficient. It was defined as 'the process of tailoring services to individual needs'. (DOH 1991b). Previously people had been offered a limited range of 'off the shelf' options and now people were to be more involved. At best this would translate the individual wishes of users into individualised services.

Take Joe for example. At 63 years old, he has been to the same day centre for 30 years. The centre was a traditional block provider. What Joe wanted was to do gardening for local people older than himself and fishing. Joe wants to help others; he does not always want to be helped, he says. He wants to fish because he used to do it with his brothers when they were children. Joe says it would be good to bring home the supper for a change! His desired gardening and fishing are not services as we usually understand them. His dreams are not difficult. He could join an angling club or local gardening volunteers.

Care management tries to transform services based on block provision to serve the extremely diverse needs of individual service users, like Joe. It is as if Next or Austin Reed, traditionally providing off-the-peg clothing, decided on bespoke tailoring – a service which measured customers choosing from thousands of different fabrics and styles.

All these obstacles go double and treble for minority groups. Stuart (1993) has coined the phrase 'simultaneous oppression' to describe how an individual may be marginalised by all groups to which he or she might belong. *'When the doctors and social workers look at me . . . they say "disabled". When I look at myself . . . I say "Black Woman". My black community leaves me on the outside because I'm disabled. My disabled community leaves me on the outside because I'm black. The doctors and the social workers . . . say is "Race" an issue for disabled people? Black people say . . . where are your nurses? . . . and why aren't you in a special place? Services are provided by white non-disabled men to white disabled men. I am a black disabled woman and services are not provided for me. Disabled groups put forward the views of white disabled people. Where am I on your pictures? These pictures tell me that disability groups are for white disabled people. I am a black disabled woman. Who puts forward my point of view?* (Gosling 1992)

Begum notes: 'The philosophy of a needs led approach is invaluable, as it provides a mechanism for ensuring that Black disabled people are not simply expected to use the services available but that care managers will put together a package of care to respond to the Black disabled person's needs.' (Begum 1995) The emphasis on the individual however is often lost in practice based on generalisations like 'what black people need is . . .' when there are many significant differences between them.

This all means a massive transformation. Morris comments: 'In general, the way in which statutory services operate is in conflict with the principles of independent living. Disabled people who have to rely solely on local authority domiciliary services are at risk of being confined to their own homes and of their personal relationships being undermined by a failure to recognise their role within their household.' (Morris 1993) The government's own principal social services adviser warned that there was still far to go before 'users, as far as possible, feel that the process is operating for them and that they have some influence on it'. (Laming 1996) Even more specifically 'one of his inspection teams noted that care planning generally appeared to be totally service-led with little evidence of flexible, innovative, individualised responses to needs identified'. (SSI 1995)

Any transformation involves providing resources in very different and largely more flexible ways – greater flexibility demands increased liquidity. One major obstacle is that existing resources are largely in buildings which are inflexible, e.g. adult training centres for people with learning difficulties exist in almost every sizeable town. These involve an investment of billions of pounds consuming gigantic fuel and maintenance costs. Developing more imaginative and creative services with flexible resources is a huge challenge especially when the drive towards individualised services thinly disguises rationing clothed in the rhetoric of cost effectiveness.

Care management is a wonderfully paradoxical process. It was imported from the United States to help ration resources in a period of rapidly expanding expenditure on social security and social services. This increased expenditure was linked with rapidly increasing inequality. Wilkinson comments: 'Most fundamentally, inequality turns a large proportion of the population from net contributors to a society's economic welfare into net burdens on it. . . . By denying people the opportunity to experience themselves as valued members of society contributing to the economy, they have no choice but to add to the social security bill.' (Wilkinson 1996 pp 225-6)

Large portions of the population are cut adrift socially and economically; people are excluded from valued ways of living. It is no coincidence that the vast majority of 'heavy end' clients are poor, or that black people are over-represented in prisons and as users of the mental health services. Nor yet that women provide disproportionate numbers of social work clients. All this reflects the way in which power is held and used in our society. (Jordan 1990)

More often than not welfare professionals find themselves negotiating the care of family members with women, since women make up most of the vast army of unpaid carers in this country. The hard daily graft of caring is encapsulated in:

I have to pull him down the bed – he is 15 stones. He holds onto the door handle while I push him up. I wash him in this position. That's me done in for the rest of the morning. The nurse who calls once a fortnight is a lovely girl but she is always in a hurry.

My ex-husband couldn't cope with it. He thought Sean should have been put in a home as soon as he was born. He said that Sean had ruined our lives. Now it's down to me and my mother lends a hand most days. I don't know what I'd do without her. The social worker got me a washing machine – they don't last long with the volume of soiled laundry we have.

I had a good job but I gave it up to look after my mother. She didn't want to be looked after by strangers and I didn't want that either. The rest of the family and the neighbours kind of assumed that I would do it. I wasn't married you see. I never imagined that at 75 I'd still be looking after her.

Practice

UK legislation does not prescribe the local authorities' implementation. There is no one practice model but a great variety. However, care management is generally broken down into eight core elements and, since people's needs change over time, best understood as a cyclical rather than a linear process.

- Publishing information
- Determining assessment levels
- Assessment
- Determining eligibility
- Care planning
- Implementation
- Monitoring
- Reviewing

Publishing information

Local authorities must publish an annual community care plan and details of complaints procedures as well as arrangements made for assessment and care management. Information should meet the particular requirements of those ordinarily marginalised by the planning processes – especially those from ethnic minorities whose first language is not English and/or where cultural attitudes are widely different from the accepted mainstream.

Determining the level of assessment

Official guidance provides six possible assessment levels ranging from simple, 'where an office receptionist might deal directly with a request for a bus pass', through to a 'comprehensive assessment involving a number of agencies'. If not handled wisely and carefully these criteria can easily develop into a bureaucratic steeplechase ending in a depressing cul-de-sac, demoralising both potential service users and direct contact staff.

Assessing need

This means assessing the needs of an individual and, if relevant, those of carers, in a way that 'recognises their strengths and aspirations'. This assessment process should be clearly distinguished from the care planning. The assessment should be 'needs led' and intended to 'objectively define needs and determine eligibility for assistance against stated policy criteria'. It is also intended to be a participative process involving the applicant, their carers, and other relevant agencies.

'Assessment is the analytical process by which decisions are made. In a social welfare context, it is a basis for planning what needs to be done to maintain or improve a person's situation, although it is not the plan itself. Still less is it the organisational arrangements which will be made to put the plan into operation, but the assessor will need to know that such arrangements are possible and acceptable. . . .' (Middleton 1997 p5)

Assessment is an unfortunate term implying a unidirectional approach by some kind of expert doing things to passive people. It seems to deny that people are experts in their own life. Assessment and care planning are fundamental to care management. The quality and efficacy of care planning are dependent on the quality of assessment.

Good assessment
  Starts with an open mind
  Starts where the individual is
  Involves and empowers the user as a partner
  Relates to their perceived problem and explores the reasons for it
  Collects only relevant data
  Puts the information in the context of its collection
  Analyses the problem using the data
  Explores the pros and cons of a range of solutions
  Thinks about a range of options
  Does not put pressure on the user to choose the option the assessor wants
  Negotiates with the individual and with existing and potential service providers, to find an acceptable and feasible solution
  Makes recommendations which relate to the information collected
  Makes arrangements for review

Bad assessment
  Diminishes the user
  Leaves too much power in the hands of the assessor
  Starts with a preconceived idea of what the solution is, or what service may be required
  Does not differentiate between individuals but puts them all through the same process
  Does not trouble to discuss individual concerns
  Does not involve the user, and may even rely on a third party or observed data only

- Relies on a tick box form as a crutch for unskilled workers
- Uses an MOT-type approach to the person, against an established view of what is normal
- Lays the difficulties at the door of the person rather than having some appreciation of their circumstances
- Talks of individual strengths and weaknesses, not aspirations, frustrations, lack of resources, or disabling environments
- Collects data for the sake of it, relating them neither to the perceived problem nor the recommended care package
- Does not explore options
- Uses no imagination
- Takes services from shelf of ready-made goods rather than creating a custom-built individual response
- Assumes the assessment has a long shelf-life and does not relate it to the time, place, and circumstances of its being undertaken. (Care Weekly 1994)

Determining Eligibility

Whatever the rhetoric, assessment is generally seen as the means by which professionals establish what the problems or issues are – looking for evidence which supports or negates their continuing involvement with the user. He/she/they may not be eligible for services. Each local authority will have devised its own criteria.

> Mrs Larkin's 21-year-old daughter Bridget has a learning disability. Bridget is still living at home and is taking an NVQ in cookery at the local college. The course finishes soon and Mrs Larkin also wants alternative accommodation for her daughter. Mrs Larkin contacts the local SSD and Bridget and her mother are assessed. From the local authority perspective there is no immediate crisis and Bridget is not at risk. The family receive advice/information about local housing agencies, college courses, employment routes, and social activities. Mrs Larkin is informed that she is not eligible for anything else because Bridget's daily needs do not place her high enough on the tariff. Mrs Larkin is given a copy of the form showing the relevant scores. Essentially Bridget is not disabled enough to receive further help.

Assessment of need does not necessarily lead to care planning because as in Bridget's case the individual/family may not be 'eligible'. This part of the care management process is a form of screening/rationing and arises because different countries, needing a passport and a change in both currency and language. Different services and professionals have different eligibility criteria, assessment systems, and jargon.

Who are the Care Managers?
Care management has been described as a quasi-profession. Care managers are frequently recruited from the traditional welfare professions. They are not necessarily social workers. Nursing and occupational therapy qualifications are common passports. Social work assistants and home help organisers may also be care managers depending on how each local authority views the necessity for a professional qualification. The rapid growth of care management contributes to the recruitment of workers without recognised qualifications, who are often less expensive.

There are skirmishes between the different professions trying to dominate or to be at the centre of this newly expanding role. There is also some confusion about what they bring to care management, viz. what they think they are doing and what are the desirable skills. For some, advocacy is paramount, listening to clients and helping them to make a case. For others, the agency dominates. Some view it as a counselling/healing experience and, for others, empowerment is crucial. Some see it as a welcome move away from traditional social work, others as a step towards it.

It is too early to gauge the staff turnover in this quasi-profession. What little is known suggests that front-line morale is very low. The stresses of care management are great; assessing, usually within a bureaucratic framework and negotiating scarce resources. People who wish to arbitrate between expressed needs, desires, and scarce resources are continually having to say NO to requests from clients and families in a world where expectations are increasing rapidly. Rationing becomes dominant.

Agency requirements are more powerful than user needs. A family may need help but may fail the eligibility criteria. Front-line staff become guardians of a new Poor Law. Care managers face service users and families daily. They become the personification of the Wailing Wall at which families plead, lament, and wail. Unlike the stone wall, dealing with and at times absorbing people's anger and pain have health implications. Staff need more support.

There is a prevailing myth in welfare professions that support comes through the supervision process or something ethereal called 'the team'. Discussion with practitioners explodes this myth. For some the maxim 'if you can't stand the heat get out of the kitchen' sums up responses from line managers. For even more despondent others, there is an uncomfortable parallel between First World War generals and troops! A NISW survey of five local authorities revealed that half the social workers did not see their main source of support as their supervisor or manager. Not being able to get people what they need was the most stressful aspect of the job. Absenteeism was a major problem in social services and in general terms; it was social workers who experienced the highest levels of dissatisfaction and frustration. (NISW 1995)

Training

A major problem in the early stages was that staff couldn't do individual care planning. They received hardly any relevant training on the professional or in-service courses. The Griffiths Report (1989) spelled out the implications for training but priority was given to managerial and organisational changes. (Levin *et al.* 1994) Traditionally, workers simply put clients into the readily available niches or onto the relevant waiting lists.

Joe needs day care so simply refer to the day care centre. This is part of a long history of inadequate, ineffective service provision. Workers are faced with a frustrating paradox of knowing this and recognising that they are too weak to bring about fundamental change. In part this is because vested interests protect the *status quo* but there is also a question of power over resources not devolved to the front line. Care management was ripe with new ideas or new ways of working but training, where it existed, reflected the needs of the agency.

Initial guidance to authorities was functionalist – care management as units of competency. CCETSW emphasises training (a narrowing down) not education or philosophy (a widening out). Training is thoroughly based on competency. This approach to training is reductionist, naïve, and simplistic. (Cannan 1995)

'Today we have naming of parts. Yesterday,
We had daily cleaning. And tomorrow morning,
We shall have what to do after firing. But today,
Today we have naming of parts. Japonica
Glistens like coral in all of the neighbouring gardens
And today we have naming of parts.'
('Naming of Parts' by Henry Reed)

In many ways we are competent and efficient. We have learnt our routines well. We put the blanket round the client . . . we make sure she is lifted appropriately and safely into the wheelchair and then into the ambulance, we fill in the correct forms *but we forget to ask why we are doing all of these things.*

It is dangerous to confuse efficiency with effectiveness – they are not necessarily the same. In medieval times, blood-letting and leeches were used very efficiently but the patient usually died. Nowadays we don't use blood-letting because we understand something about the circulation of the blood. We do sometimes use leeches even in the modern NHS, because we've learnt about their antiseptic action. There is much more to effectiveness than mere competency, more to using a rifle than just naming its parts.

Models
Five Contemporary Models
- management models focusing on the relationship between assessment care planning and budget planning
- administrative models emphasising budgetary planning and management
- advocacy models negotiating a pathway through the care system with service users
- clinical models involving direct therapeutic involvement
- empowerment models focusing on community networking to change welfare systems in line with user need.

(Biggs and Weinstein 1991)

Necessarily these broad models caricature an infinitely complex situation. They represent widely conflicting forces. These struggle to reduce overall expenditure; to shape and plan from the bottom down; to involve users and 'carers' in constructing a better life from the bottom up; to transfer real power; to heal and make whole; to help people become part of a genuine community.

These gigantic forces are harnessed with great difficulty. The needs of the agency can be overwhelming. Ryan and Newton in a study on mental health: 'The idea that care manager and client engage in a collaborative discussion about the client's needs, discuss options and agree a plan in an equal partnership appears to be largely misguided. A proportion of clients do not engage in the process at all, and many of those who do, are not understanding the process they are engaged in.' (Ryan and Newton 1996)

One problem is massive bureaucratisation. Bleach argued that community care assessments were drowning in expensive paperwork. (Bleach 1993) 'The process is often problem-oriented and is familiar and depressing to clients.' The mountain of paper is mainly about accountability and eligibility rather than empowerment. The hungry needs of the agency drown out the small voice of clients and 'carers'. Recent research indicates that the increase in bureaucracy threatens to change the whole nature of social work practice. One service manager said: 'The whole thing is about the "form", not about assessing people and determining their needs. It is about the form.' (Lewis *et al*. 1997) Another counted 23 forms relevant to care management in her department.

Some comments from care managers are:–

Some things are too personal to categorise.

Why can't we write the things relevant to the individual rather than follow headings?

Where can I write that Sarah is a stonking dancer and is desperate for a sexual relationship?

My manager agrees the forms are crass but if we don't fill them in we don't get the money.

If I have to complete one more risk assessment I'll scream.

I always apologise to clients in advance about the forms.

You should try writing your needs using this format.

There are so many forms we were given a guide on which ones to use and how to fill them in.

I never take the forms with me when I visit people, I fill them in later.

Does anybody really read them?

Forms can pathologise. They 'reduce' people's lives into various segments. We think of our life as a whole not usually in terms of components. Bureaucracy smothers creativity and is an effective block to really getting to know someone rather than clientising and servicing. We are many a mile off celebrating the person.

By the time the user has worked through the form with the worker he or she is bored and tired and feeling more like a bundle of deficits than a person with potential *to*. . . . Curiously other forms of pathologising take place. Normal and understandable feelings and emotions are disguised . . . loneliness becomes depression . . . there is a service for depression but not for loneliness. We are still describing those needs we can meet, perhaps it is too bleak to do otherwise.

Visions and Nightmares?
The aim of planning is to identify the best ways of meeting needs identified at assessment. Sadly, local authorities struggle to meet needs – hopes, dreams, and desires seem a long way off. Interestingly but perhaps not surprisingly, given the lack of training, the Social Services Inspectorate discovered a lack of clarity among some staff about the purpose of a care plan. Staff in all the authorities

visited still experienced difficulty in separating out the assessment of need from the negotiation of the care plan and were strongly tempted to link specific needs to known services without any consideration of possible alternative ways of achieving objectives.

Hudson outlines 16 long and wearisome steps in care management. These include

- setting priorities – assessment should have prioritised user needs
- explore resources of users and carers – user strengths may compensate for some difficulties
- carer resources should be examined but demands must be realistic
- define service requirements – intervention should be targeted as precisely as possible on identified needs
- consider alternatives – the care plan should not be matched with 'off the shelf' services
- discuss options – especially with carers and users; establish preferences – attempt to offer a genuine choice of service options.

(Hudson 1993)

Most steps could involve a genuine improvement in the existing process. For example, moving away from 'off the shelf' solutions and creating services which are expressly designed for an individual involve something genuinely positive. However, some still sound like a new technology, a fresh paternalism with the professionals still dominant. Terms like 'realistic' and 'prioritisation' ring alarm bells. 'Prioritise' and 'eligibility criteria' are posh words for rationing.

Local authorities have mostly spawned a mechanistic approach rather than any major shift for users. Hunter differentiates between reforms which are an example of 'technical politics', improving existing structures and systems, and 'breakthrough politics' which 'presages substantial change' The reforms are put forward as an example of 'breakthrough politics' with individualised services and the development of the mixed economy. Others, however, argue that the reforms are essentially examples of 'technical politics'. (Hunter and Ellis 1993)

Care management should mean an essential transfer of power from professionals to service users and carers. Without that transfer it becomes a cosmetic process. There are some worrying signs and few positive omens. User groups report that carers and people with disabilities notice few differences under the new system.

Standard assessment pro formas distort the dialogue and perceptions of both parties. Means generally prefigure ends. Similarly the questions we ask determine the answers obtained. We have yet to see a form which says, 'Why do you get out of bed every day? What does growing old mean for you? Are you afraid of dying?' These are questions from a human, rather than an organisational, perspective that we'd want to ask of others. At worst, these questions are not asked at all.

For the majority of people 'subject' to care planning the outcomes may not be significantly better than previous models. It is also naïve to assume it is only service professionals who can care plan. Tell that to the mother who has cared for her son for 50 years!

Other users are 'doing it for themselves'. 'Direct Power', for example, is the culmination of two years' practical work at Community Support Network and Brixton Community Sanctuary in south London. Alan Leader, co-ordinator of Lambeth Community Care, feels that no matter how flexible professionals try to be, care plans are inevitably designed to an 'institutional' social model which has little to do with the needs of the user. He has designed a resource pack for people who want to develop their own care plans and support networks; the pack helps users define, identify, and assess their own needs. The pack is user friendly with simple, clear, and concise guidance. It helps people identify alternatives to the conventional options. Leader says that professionals need to be aware that users are not just concerned with mental health services, they are often jobless, living in poverty, and in poor accommodation. (Leader 1995)

References

Begum Nasa *Care Management and Assessment from an anti-racist perspective* 1995 Social Care Research Findings Joseph Rowntree

Biggs S. and Weinstein S. Assessment, *Care Management and Inspection in Community Care* CCETSW 1991

Bleach Andrew 'Top of the Form' *Community Care* 23 Sept 1993

Brandon David and Atherton Kate 'A Brief History of Social Work in Britain' Anglia Polytechnic University 1997

Braye S. and Preston-Shoot M. *Empowering Practice in Social Care* 1995 Open University Press

Cannan C. Enterprise Culture, professional socialisation and social work education in Britain *Critical Social Policy* 14 (3)

Care Weekly 20 Jan 1994

Clarke & Lapsley Department of Health and the Welsh Office 'Social Services: Achievement and Challenge' CM 3588 March 1997

Cnaan R. 'The New American Social Work Gospel: case management of the chronically mentally ill' *British Journal of Social Work*, 24, pp533-57, 1994

Department of Health, Social Services Inspectorate 'Care Management and Assessment – Practitioners' Guide HMSO 1991

Faulkener A. *Community Care* 8-14 Sept. 1994 'Mission Impossible' Hutton W. 'The State We're In' Jonathan Cape 1995

Gosling J. *et al.* 'Presentation 29: Advocacy in Action Collective' in *INFORM '92* 'Meeting the information needs of disabled people in Europe', Dept. of Health 1992

Griffiths R. 'Agenda for Action' HMSO 1988

Hall John T. *Social Devaluation and Special Education* Jessica Kingsley 1997

House of Commons Social Services Committee *Second Report on Community Care with special reference to adult mentally ill and mentally handicapped people* (HC 13 1984-5) HMSO 1985

Hudson B. *The Busy Person's Guide to Care Management* Social Services Monographs 1993

Hunter and Ellis quoted in Holland R. *Assessment and Care Management* 1994 Unpublished MA manuscript University of Kent

Hutton W. *The State We're In* Vintage 1995

Jordan B. *Social Work in an Unjust Society* 1990 Harvester` Wheatsheaf p5

Kingdon D. Care Programme Approach Recent government policy and legislation *Psychiatric Bulletin* 18 68-70

Laming H. 'Large Retailers can provide model for care management' *Care Plan*, p7, September 1996

Leader A. *Direct Power* MIND/Pavilion 1995

Levin *et al.* NISW Social Work and Community Care: An exploratory study of the impact of recent policy changes on practitioners and managers quoted in *Issues in Social Work Education* Vol. 16 1996

Lewis Jane *et al.* 'Implementing Care Management: Issues in relation to the new Community Care' *British Journal of Social Work* vol 27, no 1, February 1997, p5-24

Middleton L. *The Art of Assessment* Venture Press 1997

Morris J. *Community care or independent living?* Rowntree 1993

NISW *Working in Social services* NISW 1995

Oliver M. *Understanding Disability – from theory to practice* Macmillan 1996

Onyett S. *Care Management in Mental Health* Chapman & Hall 1992

Poor Law Commission *Majority Report* HMSO 1909

President's Commission on Mental Health: *Report of the Task Force on De-institutionalisation, Rehabilitation and Long Term Care*, vol II 256-378 Washington DC 1978

Ramon S. 'Principles and Conceptual Knowledge' in S. Ramon (ed) *Beyond Community Care, Normalisation and Integration Work* Macmillan 1991

Reed H. 'Naming of Parts' in *The Voice of War* V. Selwyn 1995 Michael Joseph Ltd

Richmond M. *Social Diagnosis*, Russell Sage Foundation 1917; footnote on p28 on the Elberfeld service in Germany *circa* 1870

Rothman J. 'A Model of Case Management: toward empirically based practice' *Social Work* vol 36, No 6, November 1991, p520-8

Ryan P. and Newton J. *et al*. *Care Management – Is it Working?* Sainsbury Centre for Mental Health 1996

Social Services Inspectorate: A *Multi-disciplinary Inspection of Assessment and Care Management Arrangements* DHSS 1995

Stuart O. 'Double Oppression: an appropriate starting point' in Swain J., Finkelstein V. French S. and Oliver M. (eds) *Disabling Barriers – Enabling Environments* Open University/Sage 1993

Taylor B. and Devine T. *Assessing Needs and Planning Care in Social Work* Arena 1993

Utting Sir Wm. *et al. Creating Community Care* Mental Health Foundation 1994

Weil M. Karls J. *et al. Case Management in human service management* San Francisco: Jossey-Bass 1985

Wilkinson R. *Unhealthy Societies – the Afflictions of Inequality* Routledge 1996

Wolfe J. *et al*. 'Care Programme Approach: evaluation of its implementation in an inner London service' *Clinical Effectiveness in Nursing*, vol 1 issue 4, 1997 (p85-91)

Wolfensberger W. *The principle of Normalisation in Human Services* 1972 Toronto, National Institute of Mental Retardation.

Chapter 2
Care Planning

Problems

Austin defines care planning as 'the process of translating assessment data into a plan of treatment or care. An evaluation of the client's life circumstances, strengths, and weaknesses as well as knowledge of community resources are used to develop a client-specific plan of services, activities, and material resources'. (Austin 1990) This dynamic process raises some very considerable dilemmas, mostly outlined in the preceding chapter.

We are moving gradually away from traditional pathological definitions, towards a social disability model, although many professionals are fearful about this considerable shift. It is a move from client to consumer; a move which rejects domination by non-disabled people. Professionals tend to be conservative and wary about handing over power despite the discontent with the institutional ways of working. 'We know best' attitudes are still strong, where ablism remains largely unrecognised and untackled.

It is still much clearer about what is being moved away than the forward direction. We are moving away from the large Victorian hospitals and the grandchildren of the workhouses – the congregated hostels, day centres, old people's homes . . . but towards what? There is little genuine consensus amongst the various stakeholders. For example, in the learning difficulties field some relatives hold onto the idea of village communities, especially designed for people with disabilities.

We are moving towards a so-called pluralistic system underpinned by a free market approach to welfare. This presents many problems. There are difficulties in formulating national standards, arising out of the immense variety of provision. It is far from clear whether genuine choices for the users and relatives are really increased under this system. Purchaser/provider structures encourage competition rather than co-operation. The supermarket metaphor is widely used but these services constitute an extremely strange shop. The products are not like bread or butter; information is strictly limited; shoppers have no plastic cards or money, until very recently; and this shop has a virtual monopoly in most towns and villages.

Rationing is vital because resources are finite and demand infinite. These very difficult decisions about relative need are couched in meaningless terms like 'prioritisation'. The process of rationing should be much more explicit and translucent rather than covert. If it is clear who decides and on what basis, then it is easier to understand and perhaps to challenge.

There is a gross tendency toward excessive utilitarianism and pragmatism yet care planning is also a process as well as an outcome. The achievement of goals is not the only measure, perhaps in many cases not even the most significant. Simply meeting together and reflecting could be inherently healing. How do you rate on a quality chart someone simply sitting at a bedside, holding a hand of a terminally ill patient until their last moment and afterwards?

The systems encourage pathological approaches necessarily accompanied by collusion between the professional and the client to maximise the case for increased services. A colleague described one variant as the 'You can't really walk – can you?' approach to assessment. A nursing colleague suggests that different numbers can decide what sorts of services are accessible. The worse the client/patient defines his or her situation, the better he or she does in the eligibility Grand National.

We can easily eschew holistic approaches and focus instead on the component parts which can never add up to the entire person. There are so many differing philosophies and principles involved in relatively new care planning. Given pluralistic realities, reaching any consensus about priorities, especially where there are a multitude of different and competing services, can be extremely difficult, if not impossible.

There has been a regrettable tendency for care management, especially in the United States, to become extremely jargonised and technicalised. These processes take it out of the understanding of most users and relatives and back into the eager hands of trained professionals – a very dangerous trend back towards traditional disempowerment. The more obscure the jargon, the more technical the concepts, the more power remains with the various professionals.

Care management, however skilful, cannot save the whales or even clean the beaches or rectify serious power imbalances. Austin suggests that case management has been oversold. 'Although it can improve care for individual clients, depending on the capacity of the local delivery system, it cannot in and of itself achieve delivery-system goals. Furthermore, case management will not alter imbalances in the delivery system, control costs with the necessary fiscal authority, create services that do not exist and improve quality of services . . .' (Austin 1990)

Four Magnets
To help focus this whole process of care planning, we (Althea and David Brandon) devised the *four magnets* to attract the various fragments of material from people's life stories. The magnets arose out of our understanding of the principle of normalisation over more than 10 years. We have used them on dozens of care plans over the last five years in SHIELD, a university agency working directly with people who have a disability, undertaking both advocacy and care planning work.

This direct work led to looking more widely at how people lived and wanted to live. That didn't easily divide up into the various professionalised categories. We wanted to look at people's whole quality of life rather than just at their user needs. Many of the services vital to the ordinary lives of people with disabilities weren't run by health and social services. For example, income and transport arrangements were often left out of traditional assessments.

A number of studies show that care management is falling down. Singh surveyed six selected local authorities and looked at the process for people with learning difficulties. Care managers complained about the shortage of time spent on both assessments and care planning because of large caseloads. In implementing care plans, managers complained about lack of resources, particularly good quality ones (especially for ethnic minorities and those with challenging behaviours), shortage of independent providers, and lack of time. (Singh 1995)

Smith, looking at his own service, found 'standardised procedures introduced to implement care management plus increased pressure on staff, have had an adverse effect on services to people with learning disabilities'. 'Most authorities have been obsessed with creating uniform procedures to meet the needs of all client groups and particularly elderly people. In doing this they have lost some of the unique features needed to meet the individual needs of people with learning disabilities.' (Smith 1995)

We wanted to work at emphasising strengths rather than shortcomings. Saleeby wrote: 'At the very least, the strengths perspective obligates workers to understand that, however downtrodden or sick, individuals have survived (and in some cases even thrived). They have taken steps, summoned up resources, and coped. We need to know what they have done, how they have done it, what they have learned from doing it, what resources (inner and outer) were available in their struggle to surmount their troubles. People are always working on their situations, even if just deciding to be resigned to them; as helpers we must tap into that work, elucidate it, find and build on its possibilities.' (Saleeby 1992)

Examine these contrasting descriptions of the young with disabilities Kim.

Professionals:	**Family and Friends:**
'He shows a moderate developmental delay at two years eight months with skills falling a little further behind due to a developmental plateau.'	'He has such a great laugh and a lot of energy.'
'He is showing a marked developmental regression.'	'He tries so hard all the time. He never gives up.'
'He has autistic tendencies.'	'He communicates so beautifully.'
	(from Murray and Penman 1996)

There is a tendency to enter what Smail calls 'a culture of disparagement'. (Smail 1993) We may disparage runaway teenagers who live homeless on the streets of London but they are certainly achieving something more considerable and taxing than a 50-mile hike over the Lake District mountains which, along with other activities, would earn a Duke of Edinburgh gold medal. Are we going to examine their vulnerability or celebrate their capacity for survival?

The uncovering of strengths 'requires a process of co-operative exploration between clients and workers; "expert" practitioners do not have the last word on what clients need'. (De Jong and Miller 1995) It also puts a strong spotlight on the manipulation of external resources rather than on the so-called culpabilities of the individual.

We wanted to keep the whole process very simple and well under the control of those using it, easily explained and understood. Many existing systems were rather desiccated, set on uncovering problems and failings rather than on celebrating diversity. They often reflected the views of relatives or professionals rather than the focal person with disabilities and written in service speak. (Smull *et al.* 1996)

There seemed to be four basic themes to all our lives, no matter who we are – professionals, service users, or relatives.

Four Magnets
CONTROL. SKILLS. PAIN. CONTACT.

These four magnets can be applied equally to the life of anyone. They aren't about symptoms, syndromes, or medical conditions. They seem to cross – reasonably readily – gender, disability, age, religious, and racial boundaries. They are (hopefully) essentially unifying rather than divisive, to remind us that we are all human.

They relate reasonably well with Goleman's seven categories outlining *emotional intelligence* except that he does not look directly at pain . . .

1. *Confidence:* a sense of control and mastery of one's own body, behaviour and world
2. *Curiosity:* a sense that finding out about things is positive and leads to pleasure
3. *Intentionality:* the wish and capacity to have an impact and to act upon that with persistence
4. *Self-control:* the ability to modulate and control one's own actions

5. *Relatedness:* the ability to engage with others based on the sense of being understood by and understanding them
6. *Capacity to communicate:* the wish and ability to verbally exchange ideas, feelings, and concepts with others
7. *Co-operativeness:* the ability to balance one's own needs with those of others in group activity. (Goleman 1996)

In the process of the care planning we have tried hard, but rarely succeeded, to

- pay close attention through good, careful, and creative listening: 'Smiley could listen with his hooded, sleepy eyes; he could listen by the very inclination of his tubby body, by his stillness and his understanding smile. He could listen because with one exception, which was Ann, his wife, he expected nothing of his fellow souls, criticised nothing, condoned the worse of you long before you had revealed it. He could listen better than a microphone because his mind lit at once upon essentials; he seemed able to spot them before he knew where they were leading.' (Le Carre 1991 p262)
- observe very closely
- be holistic rather than partial and pathological. People are always much more than just a list of syndromes, however complex. The nature of people is always more important than the nature of their problems
- help people understand the vast labyrinth of professionals and services and sometimes the competing ego battles
- believe in and act on the rights of people with disabilities
- put them first
- steadfastly oppose a massive professional colonialism which thinks it 'knows best'
- seek out and provide information both concretely and clearly, avoiding jargon which hinders fuller involvement
- work under the direction of people with disabilities
- skilfully advocate and negotiate for improved services
- confess ignorance and learn from mistakes
- talk with and listen to relevant keyworkers, relatives, and many others in seeking more knowledge
- believe in the potential of all people despite what their casefiles might record.

We believe that care planning necessarily involves a great deal of mutual respect. It means treating the person as an active citizen rather than as a passive client/patient. It assumes that people can understand rather than that they cannot. It means recognising people's individual and unique needs.

It accepts that for many people with disabilities the existing systems have been both destructive and devaluing. Professionals have often been bossy and oppressive. We have tried to avoid the use of blaming and discriminating terminology like

- 'challenging behaviours'
- 'poorly motivated'
- 'immature'.

We have tried to involve the person at every stage and give them the time and space to work through the relevant issues. We recognised that the plan worked on is about their life and that we are leaving after a fixed series of sessions.

We tried to go through the different stages

- listening intently
- making suggestions
- taking instructions
- recording precisely
- recommending concretely
- implementing practically
- reviewing efficiently.

CONTROL

This asks basic questions about whether or not people have meaningful control over their lives or even want it? Is the pursuit of personal power encouraged? What does it really mean to be in control and to take increasing responsibility?

These are extremely complex questions. Existing services have frequently encouraged parents and service users to be dependent and passive, to be fearful of autonomy. They have discouraged people with disabilities from being active and demanding. There is a broad and important distinction between giving up control at some levels and never having had it in the first place. Some professionals treat patients and clients with disrespect, verging on contempt.

Care Planning

Jean-Dominique Bauby, paralysed by a massive stroke and only able to communicate through blinking his left eye, comments on his Berck hospital ophthalmologist. 'As the weeks went by I wondered whether the hospital employed such an ungracious character deliberately – to serve as a focal point for the veiled mistrust the medical profession always arouses in long-term patients. A kind of scapegoat, in other words. If he leaves Berck, which seems likely, who will be left for me to sneer at? I shall no longer have the solitary and innocent pleasure of hearing his eternal question, "Do you see double?" and of replying – deep inside – "Yes, I see two assholes, not one".' (Bauby 1997)

Themes of feeling powerful, feeling influential
- what you feel and think have some impact on the world, changes things
- gaining the freedom to make mistakes
- listened to carefully by relatively powerful others
- possessing the relevant information
- choosing between various options
- changing your mind

making the real decisions about
- Holidays
- Food and drink
- TV and radio programmes
- Activities
- Sex, drugs, rock 'n roll
- Relationships
- Music – from the Spice Girls to Oasis to Mozart
- Clothes
- Personal style
- Where and with whom you live.

Are you able to . . .?
- express likes and dislikes freely
- get taken notice of
- be treated – age appropriately

- get transport to attractive places.
- control your money to buy whatever is desired and can be afforded
- be seen as worthy of respect
- assume appropriate responsibility
- be seen as a valued person like others
- appoint support staff
- be involved in planning their services
- fully participate in society
- be a complete citizen rather than a client/patient
- be treated with dignity and respect.

The dignity of risk

Risk assessment processes in many services can be a straitjacket.

Do you make the major decisions in your life?

What choices? Many or few?

Do you choose with whom to spend your life?

Are you helped to gain more control over yourself?

Does the whole care planning process give people a clear and positive experience of their own control and power?

JIM *is African-Caribbean and likes clubbing more than anything else. In the dancing and loud music he comes really alive. Of course it takes place mainly in the late evenings and needs group home staff to accompany him. Risk assessment procedures state that two staff should go because of some 'challenging behaviour' in the past when he lived in a large mental handicap hospital. Staff shortages mean that it is over a year since Jim went clubbing. He cannot do what he likes most to do.*

Especially in the West, control is seen as extremely desirable, gaining power over the inevitable uncertainties. Expanding both our choices and resources is perceived as a major way of extending personal control. Money is important mainly as a means to extend this power.

For very many, love is vitally important. It helps to give real meaning to ordinary daily living; that we love and are also loved in return. Reciprocity. It usually involves some sadness – for example, thousands of the folk and pop songs are about unrequited love. And yet love largely involves feeling out of control. We become in an important way, willingly or unwillingly, under the control of the other, under their spell – the object of our love. Falling in love.

What the other does and says becomes all important. The films, poems, and songs express this intensity well. They sing of being under the control of someone else; obsessed by their voice; waiting for their letters and phone calls; staring at the photographs; hungry for the presence; remembering pleasant and sometimes unpleasant times together. Anything else in our lives can lose substance. Where there were two, there is now only one, an essential union, very painful and isolated when apart.

> 'You have ravished me away by a power I cannot resist; yet I could resist until I saw you; and even since I have seen you I have endeavoured often "to reason against the reason of my love".' (John Keats 'Letters to Fanny Brawne', (160), 13 October 1819)

Many other aspects of human activity, especially those involving taking risks, illustrate this major paradox. We gamble both with ourselves and with others. Frequently it is very difficult to calculate precisely what the existing odds are. In a way that seems the central point, to get extremely close to the edge of impermanence, of being totally overwhelmed, to be in the hands of fate.

- Taking drugs: ecstasy, alcohol, smoking – losing control, being taken over.
- Fairground rides: whirling round and round, up and down, out of control, close to and over the boundaries of fear.
- Betting: money on the national lottery, horse-racing, card playing, not knowing what is going to happen.
- Dangerous sports: bungee jumping, abseiling, mountaineering, russian roulette, risking injury and even death.

Control represents a sort of circle. The psychoanalysts write of the 'omnipotent phase' of the young child; feelings of immense power usually soon replaced by feelings of fragility and vulnerability. The drive for increased control and power is also partly, on some other layers, a pursuit of union – a sort of merging – what analysts call (often somewhat dismissively) symbiosis; the central core of spirituality. There is an important struggle between the *power of love* and the *love of power* in our lives, to which the New Testament is a powerful witness.

The sado-masochistic feelings in a great many of us are evidence of that heady mixture of pain, power, and powerlessness – especially in the areas of human sexuality. We may want both to control and to be controlled.

SKILLS

This magnet asks questions about how people are encouraged to develop personally, increase in both confidence and competence. What relevant resources and opportunities are provided? Usually services have provided little to assist the development of people with disabilities, seeing them as non-achievers.

There is usually a great benefit in feeling that something is done well in the eyes of self and others. 'What do you do?' is an important opening question to help in exploring each other. People respect the valued skills possessed by others. The extremely moving Australian film 'Shine' recounts the story of the pianist David Helfgott and his psychiatric breakdown, emphasising his recovery when accepted as a gifted pianist in a café.

Skills fall into three broad categories.
- Personal
- Social
- Activity

Personal skills
Self-control, ordinary valued structure of daily routines and discipline; possessing assurance and the elusive 'confidence'; developing insight and deepening self-awareness; effective time management; ability to handle stress adequately; ability to ask for help; the symbols and fragments of individuality. The foundation of all this is a studied and consistent reflectiveness.

Social skills
Ability to relate to others; to communicate with sensitivity and accuracy; to express oneself effectively and appropriately; capacity for empathy; to be warm and friendly and the opposite; to be assertive and to say 'NO'; to have fun and love; to enjoy yourself; to have integrity and cohesion in the eyes of others; to feel part of a team in some way, working together. Goleman puts attunement at the very heart of social skills: empathy – a feeling for others. (Goleman 1996)

Activity skills
Skills in activities are important ways of relating to others. They are valued by others, gain the perceived competent person respect. There is a marvellous scene in 'One Flew Over the Cuckoo's Nest'. A group of escaped psychiatric patients are on a fishing boat when one gets the shakes. McMurphy, the leader of the group, cries out : "Stop it. You're a fisherman now, not a lunatic."

A central way of getting to know something about people, to make enduring connections, is through shared interests; acquiring skills in some areas, becoming competent at work; being part of a team, in a variety of activities like sport, pastimes, hobbies, and leisure pursuits . . .

- playing piano
- dancing
- speaking a foreign language
- public speaking
- playing football
- cooking
- sailing
- sewing
- driving
- playing cards
- snooker/pool
- possessing valued skills at work
- computing.

Mary has Downs Syndrome and is short and stocky. On the dance floor, she is transformed into elegance and rhythm, taking part in many regional competitions. People admire her graceful movements and those of Barry, her regular dance partner, to mainly South American music. She is well known locally and people talk to her about the various competitions and perceive her as extremely competent.

Possessing and improving skills assist greatly in the growth of self-worth and confidence; in being seen as worthwhile, deserving respect from others; in self-discipline and self-expression; in relating effectively to others; being seen as dynamic, as constantly changing, growing, and improving – acquiring more skills at a more competent level as time goes on.

Curiously as we get more skilful in the eyes of others, we sometimes feel much less so. There is a loss of self-consciousness so that all the energy is concentrated on doing – what the Chinese call non-action – being totally at one with what is happening. In Zen Buddhism this feeling of knowing hardly anything and having no skills is called 'Beginner's Mind'. Along with it we become humbled and more appreciative of the endless shores of knowledge, how infinitely much there is to know. There is an old sailing dictum: 'When you are skilled enough to really sail, you are too old to do it.'

There is a sort of learning which is really unlearning. This may involve giving up some knowledge we thought we had. Meditation is a powerful method. This is usually rather more painful than acquiring so called new knowledge and skills. We can become aware that these skills simply use forces of which we are just a small part and not controlling. We feel inspired and taken over. But as George Eliot suggests, it needs both the inspiration and the person.

> 'Tis God gives skill,
> But not without men's hands; He could not make
> Antonio Stradivari's violins
> Without Antonio.'
> (George Eliot Poems: Stradivarius, 1. 140)

PAIN

This asks questions about whether the pain of different individuals is sensitively accepted and recognised. Is people's suffering seen in fundamentally human ways, recognising our commonality, rather than wrapped up in professionalised jargon and ideologies? Pain as a term appears so rarely in literature that it indicates some sort of basic denial by the professionals.

> '... Horatio, what a wounded name,
> Things standing thus unknown, shall live behind me.
> If thou didst ever hold me in thy heart,
> Absent thee from felicity awhile,
> And in this harsh world draw thy breath in pain,
> To tell my story.'
> (Shakespeare 'Hamlet' v, ii 358)

Much of the suffering by people with impairments is unnecessary. The social disability model holds that 'serious illness and physical or intellectual impairment exist but only become disabling because of the rejecting and oppressive response to such impairments by the non-disabled world'. (Hall 1967)

Suffering is a crucial part of nearly everyone's story. We need to understand it, to understand something of the lives of others. Denying the evidence of pain is to reduce others as well as ourselves. Imagine trying to understand either Hamlet or Lear without knowing that they are both driven men, tortured by what is happening to them. It would be entirely laughable.

Pain involves feelings of disease; a sense of impermanence; feelings about getting older and losing capacities, especially memory, dying and death, colds and influenza; coughs to rigor mortis; general discomfort, toothache, earache, lumbago and rheumatism, depression, despair, loneliness, confusion and being 'lost'.... Feelings of being isolated and cut off; of becoming a non-person; echoing states of fear and anxiety; friends and relatives getting ill and dying.

Psychological, physical, and spiritual suffering; struggling against often-overwhelming lusts and desires; battling for some order in our ordinary everyday lives; fear of chaos; becoming victimised and abused by others; being patronised, treated like a small child.

Struggling to make sense of pain; to try to reduce and minimise the suffering; to follow back to primary causes; to see the learning in it. Trying to reach for joy and love; for some harmony with the universe; to avoid becoming split off and alienated.

Intense suffering can drive us inwards and cut us off from those who love us. They are or seem estranged. Clare who spent most of the latter part of his life in a lunatic asylum wrote:–

> *'Into the nothingness of scorn and noise,*
> *Into the living sea of waking dreams,*
> *Where there is neither sense of life or joys,*
> *But the vast shipwreck of my life's esteems;*
> *And e'en the dearest – that I love the best –*
> *Are strange – nay, rather stranger than the rest.*
> (John Clare 'Selected Poems' Everyman 1965 p297)

In what ways do the services assist in this creative process or are part of the problem? Do they provide an atmosphere of 'realistic optimism'? Are the staff spiritually aware and sensitive about what it means to be human both for themselves and for those whom they are supporting?

Tendency to run away from or ignore the suffering and pain – both our own and others; to avoid and escape; drowning in drink, drugs and rock 'n roll, endless socialising or isolation . . . the flight from pain often turns into a flight towards it.

> What is the nature of suffering for all of us?
> How far are the support and services a source of pain?
> What help is given to understand?
> How is growth encouraged from ordinary pain to joy?
> Dealing with dying and death?
> What is the role of beauty and joy?

We talked once with staff at a Lancashire training centre who couldn't accept the grief of a man with learning difficulties. They couldn't empathise with Sam's loss of both his father and mother within six months. He'd had to move out of his home into a local authority hostel. One year after, staff felt either that he should be through the pain by now or that 'People with Down's Syndrome don't grieve'. Sam struggled not only with the loss of the two people who meant the most to him as well as his comfortable home, but also with the emotional rejection from the support workers, who were constantly trying to 'cheer him up, get him out of the sulks'.

'An inability to recognise the person's grief will make them lonely at the very time that they need other people and love and friendship. They not only need their grief recognised, they also need permission to grieve, especially if they live in a large institution where so many of the activities that take place are a sort of whipped-up happiness. It would seem that a flight into jollity is often used as a means of stifling grief by staff who do not know how to help bereaved people.' (Oswin 1991 p 30)

The effects of illness and physical pain can also be missed or misinterpreted. In Dirren's case he became angry and threw some crockery against the kitchen wall. He was sent to his room. His anger and distress continued and support workers eventually called the psychologist. Dirren's behaviour however had a physical cause, nothing to do with his disability. Later on that week Dirren was admitted to hospital for treatment for an ulcer.

Other people's fears are much like our own. There is a tendency to turn away and avoid them. Another way of avoidance is through intellectualisation and detachment from the suffering of the other. We can learn to look at people as if through a glass screen. Much personal growth and love is needed to work in more-involved, creative, and constructive ways. Most frequently we are asked to be advocates and witnesses.

Habitually we put ourselves in the way of pain; even in concrete ways like smoking or drinking to excess. These ways frequently take us 'out of control'. We like to flirt with danger by increasing the risk of injury to ourselves; we can feel that sometimes in the way we drive a car. Our psychology colleagues talk of sado-masochistic elements in personality. We can 'enjoy' a kind of suffering; just watch a suffering jogger on the road pursuing health, running through the pain barrier: the popular 'no pain no gain' philosophy.

So much of what we do is damaging. We are continually losing contact with our essential nature in steering too close to pain. The concept of 'internal saboteur' is useful. We can easily become our own 'worst enemies'. For some, the regular experiencing of pain is one of the very few ways in which to be reassured of our very existence. Much of helping involves facing the suffering and hypocrisy so prevalent in our society. This can be overwhelming, especially if we have very little emotional support.

But pain and suffering can also come close to humour. Bauby writes after his massive stroke: 'Whereupon a strange euphoria came over me. Not only was I exiled, paralysed, mute, half dead, deprived of all pleasures and reduced to a jelly-fish existence, but I was also horrible to behold. There comes a time when the heaping-up of calamities brings on uncontrollable nervous laughter – when, after a final buffet from fate, we decide to treat it all as a joke.' (Bauby 1997)

CONTACT

This asks questions about whether people are encouraged to have fun and sensuality. Are they helped to like and to love? Many people with disabilities grow up in the congregated and segregated worlds of special schools, hostels, and group homes. They don't get to know people who are not disabled. They are seen as weird and sometimes even frightening, not as potential friends and lovers.

Contact involves the whole vast range of connections with other people and pets in both quantity and quality. They can be divided into five major categories:–

- Attachment and intimacy
- Social integration
- Nourishment
- Reassurance of worth
- Reliable assistance

(Weiss quoted in Michael Bayley's 'What price Friendship?' Hexagon Press 1997)

Paid/unpaid links. How many existing connections are with professional staff who are paid and responsible primarily to an agency? They sometimes describe themselves as paid friends – a very curious combination of terms. The core of a close relationship is without cash connections. What happens when staff move to another job or go on a social work course? Do they continue the relationship?

'An open foe may prove a curse,
But a pretended friend is worse'
(Thomas Gray Fables xvii 'The Shepherds Dog and the Wolf' 1. 33)

How do we increase the numbers and depth of unpaid relationships? How many involve genuine closeness and intimacy? Warmth, relationships from the casual and superficial to the long term and deep?

- loving
- liking
- appreciating
- caring for
- being cherished
- sharing confidences
- having secrets

To what extent are these relationships truly reciprocal, the genuine sharing by equals? How many are unreciprocal and indicate a serious power imbalance? How many people can be rung at 4 a.m. and asked for help – one test of true friendship? Sensuality, sexuality. Loving and liking. From walking on air to despair; joy to sadness; dealing with being left and rejected. Fun and enjoyment: issues of quality and depth. Tears and sadness.

> 'A night without a morning,
> A trouble without end,
> A life of bitter scorning,
> A world without a friend.'
> (John Clare 30 June 1849)

Sam lost both parents and his home and was compelled to live in a disabled world, alongside 25 other residents with learning difficulties. He had to give up his real world of newspaper delivery, support from his parents, going for week-ends to his aunt and uncle, enjoying the fishing with his near neighbour, for a world where all those around were either paid or disabled. The professionals didn't accept his suffering. He found it a very lonely setting, even though the hostel was only two miles from where he was brought up. It might as well have been 100 miles.

In our conversations in the toilet (the only private space) he told me about feeling depressed and the thoughts of dying. 'I want to be in Heaven with my Mum and Dad. I don't want to carry on here.' His new life in the hostel with the prospect of moving to a group home had no real meaning for him. Eventually Sam got some counselling and felt a little better but still misses the pigeons. His Dad had a loft and enjoyed racing them with his son. They were either sold or given away after the deaths.

Contact means feeling valued by others, belonging to, recognised by, feeling identity with, respected by, others; being a member of a variety of clubs, organisations, and informal bodies:–

> Madonna fan club
> Manchester United supporters
> Rotary club
> leisure centre
> swimming club
> political party
> local church
> supper club

How are meaningful and enduring relationships made? How many are real friendships? Are relationships equal and reciprocal? Do people give and take? What is the quality of these relationships? What is the whole social network of supporters, friends, relatives, lovers, casual acquaintances, other people with disabilities. . . . ?

Bertrand Russell writes of an encounter with Joseph Conrad: ' . . . At our very first meeting, we talked with continually increasing intimacy. We seemed to sink through layer after layer of what was superficial, till gradually both reached the central fire. It was an experience unlike any other that I have known. We looked into each other's eyes, half appalled and half intoxicated to find ourselves together in such a region. The emotion was as intense as passionate love, and at the same time all embracing. I came away bewildered, and hardly able to find my way among ordinary affairs . . .' (Quoted in Hobson 1985 Pge 276) These two lonely geniuses, the novelist and the philosopher, found an intimacy within one another, unlike any previous experience.

Too much contact with others can damage one's health as easily as too little. Perhaps it should carry a government health warning! I once heard the poet Philip Larkin talk about not reading too much poetry because it would obscure his own voice. In the same way, perhaps insufficient solitude can hinder the uncovering of our own true nature. Wordsworth wrote of the 'self-sufficing power of solitude'. ('The Prelude')

Many people with disabilities live in a goldfish bowl with very little privacy. Their private and intimate business is known to many. 'In a culture in which interpersonal relationships are generally considered to provide the answer to every form of distress, it is sometimes difficult to persuade well-meaning helpers that solitude can be as therapeutic as emotional support.' (Storr 1989 p29)

We need to be alone with ourselves, to find our own space, as well as in spending time with others. The fashionable emphasis on the social nature of human beings, especially in counselling and psychotherapy textbooks, can obscure the genuine need for being on our own. We also need some space for personal healing and reflection as well as close proximity with others. Sometimes, absence really does make the heart grow fonder.

* * * * * *

Care planning necessarily involves a struggle between the needs of the particular employing agency and those of the different individuals. Advocacy is a major component of this process. The professional not only has to listen and witness but also to represent. He or she must magnify the view of the service user.

People with disabilities ordinarily face extreme odds. They are only a small if vital part of a huge industry which uses them as products and has developed very largely without their participation. This industry amplifies their social devaluation and further stigmatises their condition. The so-called service users are beginning to reformulate the traditional 'realities' created by the powerful, and the usually professional, others.

Take Aidan Shingler, labelled a schizophrenic, who has just completed a giant golden triptych in Durham Cathedral. 'Aidan Shingler is a schizophrenic artist. He's not an artist who happens to be a schizophrenic, he is an artist whose work explores and explains his state of mind. Shingler says he's not easy with the title artist and tucks a hand into his black waistcoat, drawing out a card with a few wave-like squiggles: "Aidan Shingler, reality tester." What does reality tester mean? Shingler has a way of pursing his lips as if they're glued, and his head rests at a thinking angle: "Well, psychiatrists test reality, that's what they say they do, but they've deluded themselves in my opinion. To have reality tested by a deluded person is imprecise. So I test my own reality. I don't need psychiatrists . . . to be fair, it's a bit of a joke".' (Hattenstone 1997)

Joyce Fletcher is a very frail 81-year-old and has lived in a local rest home since her husband died about five years ago. Giving up her own home involved losing large segments of *control* and autonomy. She has meals at the regulation times; goes to bed when the staff can find time to wash and undress her; can't get out to the country as often as she'd like. The staff member taking the major responsibility, she doesn't like much. She is much too coarse and rough and often treats Joyce like some naughty child. The home makes the major decisions in her life almost without her active participation. She doesn't want to be a bother.

The development of senile dementia and arthritis has meant the loss of many *skills*. She can't get dressed by herself any more; finds it difficult to walk unaided and often forgets where she is going; can't play the piano. Much of her great facility with languages (formerly head of a languages school) is being gradually erased.

Her long days, spent mostly in the bedroom, are full of *pain*. When not in the bedroom, she sits in the lounge surrounded by other residents, waiting for death, watching meaningless TV programmes. She has great stiffness and soreness from the arthritis, especially in the mornings. 'It takes me such a long time to get going after getting out of bed.' She's depressed from the gradual deterioration physically and psychologically. She is especially distressed about the loss of memory. 'My dear – you are your memory after all.'

As she gets older more of her friends and relatives die. Her *contacts* are getting fewer. She can't write letters; uses the phone only with considerable difficulty. Her visitors dwindle in numbers and frequency because seeing her distresses them so much: 'I'm not at all the person I used to be. If you had known me in those days. . . .' The various visits tend to be confined to Christmas or birthdays.

References

Austin C.D. 'Case Management – Myths and Realities' Families in Society: *The Journal of Contemporary Human Services* (pp398-405) 1990

Bauby J. D. *The Diving Bell & the Butterfly* Fourth Estate 1997

Brandon D. and A. *Yin and Yang of Care Planning* Anglia Polytechnic University 1993

De Jong P. and Miller S.D. 'How to interview for Client strengths' *Social Work*, vol 40, no 6 (p729-36) Nov 1995

Goleman D. *Emotional Intelligence* Bloomsbury 1996

Hall J. *Social Devaluation and Special Education* Jessica Kingsley 1997

Hattenstone S. 'Mind over Matter' *The Guardian*, 23 Aug 1997

Hobson R. F. *Forms of Feeling – the heart of psychotherapy* Tavistock/ Routledge 1985

Le Carré J. *The Secret Pilgrim* Coronet 1991

Murray P. and Penman J. (Compilers) *Let our Children be* Parents with Attitude 1996

Oswin M. *Am I allowed to cry?* Souvenir 1991

Saleeby D. (Editor) *The strengths perspective in social work practice* Longman (New York) 1992

Singh P. *Community Care: Britain's other lottery* Mencap report 1995

Smail D. *The Origins of Unhappiness* Harper Collins 1993 (p193)

Smith K. 'Individual needs swamped by tide of demand' *Care Plan*, Sept 1995 (p7-9)

Smull M. W. *et al. Reviewing essential lifestyle plans: criteria for best plans* University of Maryland, USA 1996

Storr A. *Solitude* Flamingo 1989

Chapter 3
Yvonne

Paul Sutton

Yvonne is a warm, lively person who likes to dress casually. She comes across as relaxed and confident. She is 41 years old, about 5ft 6in tall with long, dark hair. She has an older sister, an artist living in Detroit in the United States. She is a direct person. 'I can't stand "bullshit". I prefer honesty.'

Yvonne was born in England but soon moved to Norway, the home of her mother, where her father farmed mink. Five years later she moved to Scotland where her father continued in the mink business. In 1964 they moved to a small, pretty Cambridgeshire village where she has remained ever since. She went to school in the area and then to college to study hairdressing. Her mother is 68, lives over the road, and suffers from emphysema. Her father was in the navy and now lives in Cornwall.

At 15, Yvonne met her husband-to-be Paul and at 17 they got married. This was the beginning of '20 years of pure bliss'. Paul was a sheet metal worker in the American Air Force. On discharge, he retrained as a carpenter. Much of his work is seen about their home. They had two sons: Eric, 24, who is a stone mason and currently working in Singapore; and Ian, 21, who works in an electrical factory in Cambridge. Eric enjoys his work but Ian is less enthusiastic. Ian still lives at home with Yvonne and both sons have helped their mother morally, physically, and financially. Eric is much missed by the rest of the family when he is away. Both sons love music and play in a band.

When the boys were born, Yvonne gave up work but continued to cut hair at home. When she returned to work it was as a cook at one of the local colleges. She enjoyed her work and was offered the job of running the kitchen on a permanent basis. She turned it down as there was enough money coming in and she didn't want the extra responsibility.

In 1993, Yvonne had a head injury as a result of a car crash in which her husband was killed. After a long period in hospital, Yvonne returned home. She no longer does paid work but attends Headway, a local resource for people with head injuries, twice weekly.

Control

Yvonne has control over everyday living arrangements. She has all her things around her, including her record collection, so she can listen to what she wishes. She is very fond of music. Going to a concert with flashing lights, as she used to, is out as it might bring on a fit. She can't drive even if she wanted to because of the epilepsy, so she needs lifts or taxis. She doesn't carry things upstairs, like the vacuum cleaner, for the same reason. Paul and Yvonne 'used to walk miles across the fields' but she no longer dares to walk alone in case of a fit. Her sons worry about this. She trusts their judgement as they 'have often been right in the past'.

When Paul was at work 'he earned good money'. Now Yvonne is limited to living off benefits and whatever help her sons can give. This considerably affects what she can afford to do. Her support worker was taken away by her social services so she pays for someone herself.

Since the injury, it has been difficult to control her weight, so she takes extra care in what she eats. She is a vegetarian. She likes to dress in her own 'comfortable style' and has been unable to replace her wardrobe to the extent she would wish following the accident.

In the past, she travelled extensively with Paul, including America, Africa, and Europe. She has climbed Snowdon and Ben Nevis with Paul and her sons. Her injuries and financial circumstances limit her travelling now.

Skills

She had to relearn everything after the head injury – 'even going to the toilet'. She has been very successful in this task. The kitchen is once again 'Yvonne's kitchen' – a tribute to her culinary skills, as a plaque on the wall says.

Yvonne is creative, reflected in the pottery made at Headway. She made pots before the accident and is really pleased that she can again. She is now a vegetarian cook with a creative flair 'matching different flavours'. She threw a dinner party and prepared a mushroom risotto for a friend who is also a cook. The party and the dish were a great success. She has gained enough strength in her arms to make pastry but has still not tackled bread.

She discovered during the course of cutting the hair of one of her carers that her hairdressing skills are still there. She has since lost her favourite scissors but will have another go when she finds them. As well as no longer being able to drive a car Yvonne has forgotten how to ride a motorbike. She remembers riding pillion with Paul and knows she had a licence. At Headway, Yvonne has learnt to use the multi-gym and keeps herself fit. She no longer swims in England but does in the United States.

Pain

The loss of Paul and their loving relationship feature largely in Yvonne's life. On the 15 December 1993 Yvonne and Paul were in the car on their way to pick up Paul's mother from Luton Airport. She had been visiting following her husband's death. On the way to the airport the car left the road and hit a tree. Paul broke his back and died. Yvonne was taken to hospital where she stayed for seven months. Her injuries were extensive including damage to many internal organs including her spleen. She has large scars on her front where surgery was done. She had a head injury and was given injections directly into the brain. She was not expected to live. She was known as 'the miracle lady'. Now she has odd aches and pains inside and some memory loss – a total blank for the accident and partial about present and past. She takes Tegretol to help prevent epileptic seizures. She had a lot of seizures at first but the last one was in November when she forgot to take her tablet.

The accident clearly brought sudden and traumatic change to Yvonne's life. 'It took a month to accept Paul being dead, that was difficult for the kids too.' This was coupled with the massive alteration and uncertainty arising from her own injuries which 'screwed her up' leaving her to 'learn everything again'. This was a time of change and pain that is central to her life. Since then she 'does not feel the same person' and has 'odd aches and pains inside'. Her memory has been damaged and she takes 440 mgs of Tegretol a day. She does not know what the side effects of the medication are and would like to find this out. She cannot do the same things as previously.

Yvonne is aware that as her sons grow up they will leave to start new lives of their own. She accepts this as natural and desirable. Eric has started with his trip to Singapore. This leaving home is harder for her than for other mothers because she has needed so much support and care from her sons during recovery. As a mother, she feels pain because Ian is very stressed at the moment.

Yvonne passed 40 last year and this was 'a big thing' for her. She can no longer drive because of the epilepsy but anyway driving is upsetting because of the accident. Last year, just a week before she could apply for her licence back, she forgot the medication and had a fit. She has to wait at least another year before reapplying. As she lives in a rural area with an unreliable bus service, she finds it hard to get about. She hasn't even been 'boogying', which is important and pleasurable.

Contact
Before the accident Yvonne and Paul were very sociable people. She still knows many people, including friends going back to schooldays. Social events are not "her bag" but concerts and gigs are. Her near neighbour is someone she worked with, so she still knows what goes on. She was invited to the Christmas party last year. Yvonne is good company. It is not difficult to imagine that people want to include her in various social activities.

She knows many people at Headway where she goes twice weekly. She shares the experience of head injury with the members. 'It is difficult for anyone else to really understand,' she comments. At Headway, Yvonne joins in most of the activities and is extremely popular. Mike, one of the multi-gym instructors, gives her a lift once a week to a village sports hall so that she can have an extra work-out.

Yvonne has a man-friend in Florida, whom she visited last year and hopes to visit again this year. He has two young children so is more tied down. Yvonne has thought about moving to the United States but is aware that she would face medical expenses because of her injury. If they ever 'get it together' it will be at some lengthy time in the future. One Headway member has shown keen interest in her but she is 'keeping him on hold at the moment'.

In the evening, Yvonne likes listening to music and there is often the sound of her youngest son mixing disco stuff upstairs. She watches anything interesting on TV or reads magazines, such as 'Woman' or 'Woman's Own'. She used to read a lot before her accident – Tolkien was a particular favourite.

Yvonne uses transcendental meditation. Sometimes she does bending and stretching exercises on the rug of an evening. She describes herself as 'basically an old hippy'.

Recommendations
- Arrange through her GP to see the consultant to find out more about her injuries and how they'll affect life in the future.
- Obtain information about epilepsy so that she can understand what has and is happening to her.
- Investigate taking advantage of 'earnings disregard' within the benefit system to see if she can earn some money without affecting current benefits.
- Her younger son is stressed. Investigate local options for counselling young people.
- A food processor may help in cooking dishes which require strength in hands and arms.
- Investigate city food shops/delis and stocks of exotic ingredients.
- Contact her social worker to see if there is an existing care plan.
- Investigate options for boogying.

Themes
- the 'before and after' dimensions in Yvonne's car crash head injury
- difficulties in getting information from a multitude of case files kept in different places and using widely varying frameworks

- many needs are not met by 'services', for example, transport and boogying.
- her sons forced almost overnight into the role of 'parents'
- importance of strong neighbourhood connections. Yvonne is well rooted in her village and didn't go away to residential care. People have known her since schooldays
- continual struggle against poverty
- problems with transport in a rural area, worsened because, with epilepsy, she can't yet hold a driving licence
- difficulties with memory, recalling aspects of life is an important aspect of identity
- the club role of Headway and mixing with people who 'know what it is like' – peer support
- burden of other people's fears/expectations, e.g. her acquired 'miracle woman' identity.

Chapter 4
Max

Annie Hawkes

'Nobody Nowhere'
"In a room without windows, in the company of shadows,
You know they won't forget you, they'll take you in.
Emotionally shattered, don't ask if it mattered,
Don't let it upset, just start again.

In a world under glass, you can watch the world pass,
And nobody can touch you, you think you are safe.
But the wind can blow cold, in the depths of your soul,
Where you think nothing can hurt you till it is too late.

Run till you drop, do you know how to stop?
All the people walk right past you, you wave goodbye.
They all merely smiled, for you looked like a child
Never thought that they'd upset you, they saw you cry.

So take advice, don't question the experts.
Don't think twice, you just might listen,
Run and hide, to the corners of your mind, alone,
Like a nobody nowhere."
(Williams 1993)

Labelled deaf, abnormal, nut, retard, spastic, mental, moron, crazy, weird, wild, and insane Donna Williams existed in a state of dreamlike recession, viewing her incomprehensible surroundings from the security of a 'world under glass'. Few people understood her, least of all Donna herself, and she yearned to become 'normal'. At the age of 25, Donna discovered a word, a new label, which brought with it a handful of answers, a chance for forgiveness, and hope for a sense of belonging – autism.

Julie Malone read Donna Williams's words and recognised her 20-year-old son, Max. This is the story of my contact with the family.

Julie Malone, was, in agency speak, a 'self-referral'. We sometimes underestimate what it takes for people to refer themselves to statutory agencies. The Malone family had resisted contact with agencies, preferring to get by without interference, or as Julie said 'the so-called help from strangers'. Contact with me was associated with failure and defeat rather than rights.

First meeting
'Red Lipstick'
Julie suggested I wear a bright lipstick. Her son Max likes bright lipstick. She said, 'He may not look at you; he makes very little eye contact but he may take more of an interest if you are wearing bright lipstick. He might decide to stay in his bedroom of course but I have told him you are coming.' Bright lipstick is not usually my style but, having wrestled with the suggestion as only a die-hard feminist could, I decided to take her advice.

Julie is a petite woman in her 50s. Her appearance belies her strength. She quickly and wearily pours out the story, crying as she does so. She has had a bellyful of the so-called helping professions when her son was younger. My inclination is to hold and comfort her but such an action would say more about *my* pain and need for comfort than Julie's.

She's at the end of her tether. Her marriage broke down a couple of years ago. She doesn't say why and I don't ask because this isn't an autopsy. Julie and Max were given temporary accommodation before they moved to the present flat. A divorce and two-house moves over two years rate high on the stress scale. Supporting Max was never easy but things have been much worse since moving to the flat.

Julie and Max's accommodation is of Lilliputian proportions. As well as space, privacy is also a problem. The walls are thin enough to hear their neighbour flush the toilet. There is a collage of photographs on the sitting room wall. Julie points to one of Max when he was little. Julie stares at the photograph saying: 'I can see now that even then something wasn't quite right.' She recognises something in the facial expression that makes sense only in retrospect. On the mantle there is also a picture drawn by Max. Julie says she has hundreds and they are all very similar – detailed drawings of fireworks, one of several things which fascinate Max. Preparations for 5 November begin early in this household. It is a season Julie dreads.

Julie is really tired. Max stays awake well into the night talking and laughing to himself. Sometimes he makes a snack – a potentially dangerous activity for he is easily distracted, something as simple as rain on the window pane can absorb him for hours. There are times, in my care planning work, when I have envied him this intense power of concentration.

Max places objects in specific places in his bedroom. Like an unspoken code, his mother can read his state of mind from various rituals, e.g. the more complex the positioning of the objects the more fearful and distressed he is. He also spends up to three hours at a time in the bathroom in private routines and rituals. Since the flat has only one toilet this is an unbearable situation for his mother. It is equally unbearable having to tell this to a stranger.

Julie says Max is frightened. His rituals make him feel safe and in some strange way in control. He knows he can't manage without them. His mother accepts these rituals unconditionally. Max is afraid others may not understand and stop him. Sinclair's words are apt: 'If you would help me, don't try to change me to fit your world. Don't try to confine me to some tiny part of the world that you can change to fit me. Grant me the dignity of meeting me on my own terms – recognise that we are all equally alien to each other, and that my ways of being are not merely damaged versions of yours.' (Sinclair 1992)

Max comes into the room. Julie goes to make a drink, leaving Max and me alone. Max sizes me up with one brief glance. He speaks quickly, without punctuation. He tells me he loves Julie and wants to marry her. He hates the flat. 'Can you help me and Julie?' he asks holding his head as if some great explosion had just happened. We speak about him leaving the family home. He would prefer to stay with his mother. Again he says, 'I love my mother and want to marry her.' This must be enormously distressing for Julie. Her laughter is brittle as she explains that can never be.

Max continues to hold his head and occasionally looks up to give me a quick look. At no time do we make eye contact. Max says he wants to share a house with a woman. If he moves he will visit Julie every day. He hates the flat; he hates living up in the sky. We are all exhausted; I arrange to meet Max again, this time in a local pub.

Mine's autism – what's yours?
A man is playing the fruit machine.
Max stands near him, too near,
coin in hand, ready, impatient for his turn.
The man says nothing but with his body
speaks to Max and the world.
Max does not know this language and so
with deaf eyes continues to press close.
As if to punish this stubbornness the man
slowly and carefully places five more coins in the machine.
The code is familiar to me but Max struggles to decipher
For him the rules of the game in the machine are much easier to comprehend.

Like others with autism, Max is stumped by complex emotions and the 'games people play'. Grandin describes this as feeling like an 'Anthropologist on Mars.' (Grandin 1995) Watching Max in the pub I began to understand.

We order some cokes. Max rubs his hands a lot and contorts his face before speaking. He looks tense. We talk about the house where he used to live and his love for Julie. Both are very important to him. He thinks he would also like to get a job. He becomes excited, rocking and rubbing his hands at the thought of moving house.

Labelling Max
Julie found diagnostic labels comforting which is common among the parents I've worked with. For Julie, the label provides an identifiable reason for Max's behaviour and a way to talk about and understand. Liberal professionals like myself, sometimes overlook the comforting aspects of labelling.

Amongst the professionals involved with the Malones there is some debate as to whether Max has autism or Asperger's syndrome. Autism was described by Kanner and Asperger in the 1940s. They looked at autism clinically. Kanner and Asperger emphasised mental 'aloneness' as the defining feature hence the name 'autism'. Another defining feature was an obsessive insistence on sameness, e.g. the need for the same rituals/routines.

In the 1970s others trained in new cognitive psychology, for example Lorna Wing developed psychological theories in which impairments in socialisation, communication, and imagination cohere (Wing 1991), commonly known amongst professionals as a triad of impairment. Wing introduced the term 'Asperger's syndrome' for the 'higher functioning' child and adult with autism. It is also suggested that people with Asperger's syndrome can describe their experiences/inner feelings, whereas those with classical autism cannot.

As for aetiology, Asperger saw it as a biological defect whereas Kanner perceived it as a psychogenic disorder – a reflection of bad parenting especially from a remote, cold mother. (Sacks 1995) Currently, mothers have been vindicated. It is widely agreed that autism is biological or genetic in cause. The incidence is around one in a thousand, most often males, and no two people with autism are the same. One unfortunate spin-off of the marvellous film 'Rain Man' is that people expect genius. Autism is most often seen as a medical condition and pathologised as a syndrome, but can also be perceived as a profoundly different identity or way of being.

With the oft-forgotten maxim 'first do no harm' in mind I thought about ways to help. I can do nothing to change Max's autism. I can't care plan it away. However, I can try and see the world though their eyes, walk a mile in their moccasins. (Kelly 1955) I also need to work out the extent to which environment exacerbates their difficulties and how amenable to change it is. There are other structures I have to deal with. The agency in which I work has its own momentum – its own rules and bureaucracy.

Over the next week I meet with Julie and Max again. There is always some anxiety when we do that I will miss the most important things, often the small things we take for granted. I've arranged a new home and support for someone but it was choosing what to have for lunch that made the difference. What is important to one may be meaningless to another. My life would be poorer without poetry but would care planners necessarily see that as a need?

I am supposed to use an assessment form with service users. The agency also provides a check-list of needs to direct the work. I find this impossible – a contradiction in terms. Dialogue is a human rather than paper exercise. It is of the flesh: eyes, mouths, hands, gestures, and, most difficult of all, a mind free to listen – these are difficult with a form in the hand. I know of other workers who have no paper conflict. Instead of feeling restrained by forms, an external order is imposed offering safety and security. This is true of most structures and whether we feel liberated or oppressed is down to our own experiences. Apostate I may be but not so foolish as to cut off my nose to spite my face. The relevant forms need filling in if the money is to be accessed. I comply with gritted teeth. Like Socrates, I look at the system and think, 'There is so much in this market place we don't need.'

Flat out

It was clear early on that the flat was a big mistake. Both Julie and Max hated it passionately. They felt claustrophobic and unable to get away from one another. The feeling of being up in the air was really difficult for Max. Julie had no garden for a retreat and the flat only had one toilet. Neighbours were difficult – understandably, for Max played music long into the night.

I learnt from Max that he liked the neighbourhood where they used to live. This was a poor, inner-city estate – the kind of area for social worker's cars but not their offices. I don't want to create a parody of East End neighbourliness or conjure up comforting ideas of wartime-extended families drinking Ovaltine BUT there was something that this family wanted back – acceptance, tolerance, a certain kind of invisibility.

The people on the estate knew Max and Julie, had seen Max around and grown used to his sometimes bizarre behaviour. They learnt all this and more gradually over the years. Julie and Max's current neighbours didn't have this strength. Maybe this is a helpful insight to all working in community care. Julie and Max's former home also had a garden as well as two toilets.

All roads pointed to a return to their old stomping ground. Julie and Max were in no condition for self-advocacy, I would advocate on their behalf.

Negotiation – art of the possible
I phoned and also wrote to the council explaining the situation; making a case for a transfer to a house with two toilets in their old area or alternatively two houses. This last request was based on the long term needs of the family to be near but to be apart. Max could not live alone so this option would mean supporting him in a tenancy . . . possibly involving the Independent Living Fund in financing a care package. He'd need support with most aspects of daily life.

There were no vacancies in existing supported living projects though sharing with others in this form of accommodation may have been difficult for both Max and his co-tenants. Living in a traditional residential home or hostel would have been impossible. Institutional rules and rhythms and above all sharing a bathroom would have been intolerable. Without support from his mother, Max could easily have become one of many homeless people with mental health or learning difficulties who fall through the net.

Stumbling block . . . money, money, money, or rather the lack of it
Julie and Max had little money. Julie could not get paid work because she had to be there for Max. They had rent arrears. She pulled a sheaf of benefit forms and letters from a collapsed stack behind a cushion. 'Pick a form, any form, there is more where these came from.' I generally try and work in ways which empower but sometimes what people really need is someone to take over and get on with it. This was one of those times. Julie was at her wits' end and what she needed was for me to take these forms away and deal with them.

Housing arrears meant they could not transfer. The council were clear that there was no way to circumvent this policy. Moses' tablets of stone were the model. There was an unusual solution. I arranged a loan from our agency to the family so the arrears could be paid. This was expedient from the agency's perspective – a point made in negotiations with management.

Max was excited at the prospect of moving back to the old estate. He wanted it happening NOW and couldn't understand the delay. As soon as he knew I was talking to the council he started to harass Julie – 'When are we moving? When? When? When?' As if this wasn't hard enough he started packing and rolling up carpets etc. Julie was going crazy and we spent hours talking on the phone; tearful outpourings on the previous day's difficulties.

Dialogue with the housing authority continued 'They can't be re-housed unless its fire or flood.' 'How about murder?' I said to the humourless official at the other end of the phone. Eventually I found someone who not only listened but gave good counsel. I prepared a long report for the next council meeting and was in regular contact with the housing officer pressing the urgency of the family's case. Three weeks in the world of council housing is not long but for Julia and Max it seemed interminable.

You are probably wondering why I did not offer the family some 'respite care', the usual service response. Julie and I did go through the options but there was nothing the agency could offer that would suit Max.

Julie was offered the tenancy of a three-bedroom house with two toilets in the area where they used to live. She accepted this though we all see this as temporary. Max will at some point need to move out or alternatively Julie. My work is unfinished. We are looking at another tenancy or renting from the private sector and recruiting support for Max. The latter would be easier but Max loves the current place and if he moves it needs to be in the same area. Julie accepts that she is always going to have to be around for Max.

Small tensile carer,
reconciled not resigned.
Herein lies the difference
The one martyred, bitter.
The other accepting what is,
yet still able to dream
of what might have been.

In the name of love
I have debated with friends the cash:love nexus. My own view is that women like Julie should receive an income for the work they do. We need to include 'paying to' and 'paying for' in the sanitised academic discussions we have around 'caring for' and 'caring about'. Direct payments may offer some hope to relatives currently working under the name of love, of receiving money. It is outdated to think otherwise. At present I am helping Julie and Max through the labyrinthine tunnels of the benefits system to add to their meagre income. Sometimes this feels the most valuable part of any assessment/care planning. Research shows that social workers are not as good at this as they think.

Care planning for friends
Both Julie and Max realise that he needs someone other than Julie to go out and feel safe with. This would go some way to easing the claustrophobic aspects of their relationship.

Friends can't be purchased and in looking at our lives we probably have few friends and many acquaintances. If community contact has a shape it's like a pyramid. The broad base is the many contacts we have, ranging from Suzie, the barmaid at the local pub, to Bert the pensioner, who lives across the street. From these different connections friendships may grow over the long term. We are considering a supporter for Max to help him make this broad range of contacts in his community.

I put Julie in contact with a local self-help group. She will be an asset to the group and it may be of more help to talk to others in similar circumstances than to professionals.

Work
Max is not going off to work yet but we are optimistic. A local agency will 'take him on their books' and see if they can find work which will suit him. Stocking up in a supermarket, which is usually done in late evening when there are fewer staff around and of course fewer customers, might be worth a try. This would be okay, Max thinks. The idea of mail sorting is also being investigated. Max believes he would be able to do this also. When he starts a job he is going to need help integrating this new activity into his existing routine. Julia will help him with this.

Cost effective for the taxpayer?
Other than the loan to pay rent arrears and my time, the family cost the agency nothing. This will change when Max moves on to a supported living arrangement. We are still wrestling with the benefits but we've obtained over £600 from various charities to help with the new house. Julie says she's not a beggar. She'd like to pay her own way but it's impossible on the money she and Max get. I was so excited at the money I forgot what it's like to be on the receiving end of charity.

The family will need nourishing over the long term. It's never going to be easy regardless of whether they live together or apart. Each situation carries dilemmas and difficulties. Forgive the mixed metaphor, but the road ahead is unlikely to be plain sailing.

Max showed no interest at all in this story. Julie thought it read like a chronicle of disaster. Somewhere in between there's been much to celebrate.

Themes
- trying to understand a different world with different rules
- problems in moving across service boundaries, different regulations and languages

- importance of relocating to a supportive neighbourhood where people know and can accept Max and Julie as people
- need to understand the vital nature of Max's rituals
- battling against bureaucracy. Negotiation with the employing agency as well as the housing authority
- problems in struggling against poverty as in the way the rent arrears prevented the move to other accommodation
- problems in making friends. Befriending schemes aim to help. But do they work?
- cost effectiveness – care plan options don't always cost the earth
- ingenuity – struggling against the well-worn service pathways to create something innovative especially designed for Julie and Max.

References

Grandin T. quoted in Sacks Oliver *An Anthropologist on Mars* 1995 Picador

Kelly G. *The Psychology of Personal Construct*s 1955 New York W.W. Norton

Sacks O. *An Anthropologist on Mar*s Picador 1995

Sinclair 1992 from *Autism - The Invisible Children*; The National Autistic Society, London

Williams D. *Nobody Nowhere* 1993 Corgi Books

Wing L. *The relationship between Asperger's Syndrome and Kanner's Autism.* In Uta

Frith (editor) *Autism and Asperger Syndrome* 1991 Cambridge University Press.

Chapter 5
Mandy

Althea Brandon

In September 1993 a care planning project called Shield was set up in Anglia Polytechnic University to train students in a direct and practical way. The purpose was to provide people with an individualised plan. There would be no conflict of interests with purchasers or providers. Four years later we have completed over a hundred plans, some fully implemented, all taken into account by the local authority and voluntary agencies. They have involved attempts to assist people to speak up for themselves. When people could not speak, many hours of observation and detective work were spent in finding out what they wanted. I have called this type of independent care planning 'assisted self-advocacy'.

Nursing students, social work students, some from Romania, Ukraine, and Slovenia on Tempus programmes have been involved. We took referrals from a variety of different sources, including some directly from families and individuals. As a freelance lecturer I have been fortunate enough to be part of this project.

We have worked mainly with people with learning difficulties and individuals with head injuries. Our approach is rooted in working towards a valued lifestyle and is relevant for most people. Most customers were living in small, staffed, group homes run by voluntary agencies and attending local authority day centres. Not surprisingly, we found that most wanted much more from their lives.

My first care plan frightened me with its simplicity. It could have been written by a child. Surely no one would take it seriously. More importantly it expressed the ordinary life and dreams of persons with learning difficulties in a language that they could understand.

Meeting Mandy

Terry Bailey asked me if I would do a care plan with his daughter Mandy. It would make recommendations which the family could consider and implement later. We discussed the four magnets and Terry was enthusiastic about this approach. He was involved in a parents' pressure group and quickly saw all its implications. He felt a new vision was needed locally.

During the months of June to August 1994, I saw Mandy at least once weekly. I also visited her day care placement. When writing a care plan it is important to meet or talk to as many people as possible who know the person and research other issues, for example medical conditions and job opportunities.

The first meeting was at my flat. Mandy and her parents came for tea. I explained what care planning was and she liked the sound of it. I had a friend from Slovenia staying at the time, there was lots of laughter, and we were invited back to Mandy's home for tea. She was very pleased to see us and we spent some time getting to know each other. By the next meeting I had written a brief description of Mandy, which I read for her approval.

'Mandy is an attractive young woman with bright eyes and lots of energy. She has fashionably short dark hair and a slim athletic build. Her manner is charming and she is friendly and well spoken. She excels at sport. She lives in a beautiful and loving environment. Mandy spends a lot of time with her mum and dad, which is fine. However she's beginning to feel the need for a break from them.'

Other details concerning her family are included in this opening to the plan. I tried to keep the language as simple as possible and explained any new words so that she could understand. A real and positive introduction to the person is important, too often we concentrate on the 'negatives' and miss the person. Imagine if we introduced public figures by concentrating on what they couldn't do and then listed their medical conditions!

Mandy liked what I'd written. I made it clear she can change anything at any time. This proved a little difficult as I'd discovered that Mandy likes to agree with what is said. We worked on this major task, helping Mandy to understand that it is her care plan, about her life. She told me her story, enjoyed watching me write down her words, and read them back.

At the next meeting when I read back her story, I was pleased to discover that she corrected me. She was delighted to see the crossing out of mistakes and the writing down of her exact words. We were now ready to look at Mandy's choices and control. The easiest way was to ask what she does in the day from the moment she gets up until bedtime. I also questioned her about likes and dislikes. We both enjoyed this, almost losing sight of the care plan. I did recall that sometimes BIG choices get lost in looking at small details so we concentrated on those.

Mandy is given plenty of choice by her parents, but is still dependent on them to run her life. The placement in the day centre was neither her choice nor her parents'. Mandy would like to be more in charge of her life.

We wrote a list of recommendations to go at the end. Arising out of the discussions about her day, we wrote: could we find a friend of her own age to go to discos and to share with? This woman could include Mandy into her own circle of friends. It would be useful if she owned a car.'

The main part of the plan states: Sometimes she may get upset and does not like people shouting. Apart from her family and their friends, she only meets other people with disabilities. She is warm and open and should easily make friends.' It struck me at the time how completely local day services had isolated a lovely, sociable young woman.

Then we looked at her skills, listing the many physical abilities she's developed. We spent much time discussing horse riding which gives her a lot of pleasure. She showed me her certificates and photos. Afterwards I spoke with her tutor at the Cambridge College of Agriculture and Horticulture. We both thought it important to continue the riding. We recommended that she extend some skills and include new ones that might help her to be more independent, for example: 'Mandy would like to collect the benefits herself. She would also like to learn about managing money.'

We discussed the idea of paid work, writing down her ideas. By this time she was saying: 'This is my life, a job that I want to do.' She was clear about wanting paid work but unsure what to do. It would have been so easy to unduly influence her. I felt this process should take some time. She needed to learn more about what was on offer and I did not want to make any promises. It is important in exploring people's dreams that you're honest. A balance must be found between a person's right to dream and what is possible.

This is true for everyone, but some people may believe that dreams will automatically come true. Mandy was capable of achieving far more than what was on offer at that time. There was no reason why she shouldn't be working but would need initial support.

Right from the start, Mandy was clear about leaving home but didn't want to hurry. We added: 'When Mandy is ready to leave home she would like to share with one other person with a disability that she liked.
    or
'Live with another person without a disability. (Lifeshare scheme.) We noted that she would need some support and wanted to live near her parents.'

Towards the end of our time, Mandy trusted me enough to share some painful experiences. She didn't want these recorded so we left them out. There were some things she was happy to include concerning some of her struggles. We noted the benefits situation at the end.

We asked her parents if they would like to hear what we'd written. They were surprised at how much Mandy recalled and at how confident she had become. She no longer looked to them to answer questions.

Care Plan
Amanda Bailey – Date of birth: 4 August 1967.
Mandy is an attractive young woman with bright eyes and lots of energy. She has fashionably short dark hair and a slim athletic build. Her manner is

charming, she is friendly and well spoken. Occasionally she may stumble over a word. She excels at sports. Horse-riding is her favourite sport. She represented the East of England for RDA, coming second in the country.

Mandy lives with her parents Terry and June and her brother Paul in a cottage flat in the grounds of Duxford Mill, where Terry and Paul are employed in building and upkeep. June helps in the garden. She runs a play group where children with special needs mix with other children. On Fridays Mandy works at this nursery.

This is a beautiful and loving environment. A sister Eileen lives in Cyprus and has two children, Jamie and Lucy. The family continues to visit them. Sam and Gemma are sister Joanne's children. Mandy is very fond of them, particularly Sam, the baby. Her other sister Diane has a daughter Marie, someone else for Mandy to love. Terry takes Mandy swimming on Monday evenings to the St Christopher Club where races and training are organised. She completed 46 lengths in one hour. Mandy spends a lot of time with her mum and dad, which is fine. However she too feels it might be nice to have a break from them at times.

Mandy was born in Greenwich and lived in Eltham, south-east London. She attended Slade special school in Woolwich until she was about 10. The family moved to Sudbury in Suffolk. She attended Hillside Special School until she was 16. At school she enjoyed all sports, especially the egg-and-spoon race. She learnt to write her name but not to read. Then she went to Bury College for three years. The family moved to Duxford and Mandy was placed in Camfields Day Centre.

Mandy is given plenty of choices by her parents but is still dependent on them to run her life. The placement in Camfields was not her choice nor her parents'. She is very aware of her likes and dislikes but eager to please. She has no real control over important issues in her life. Terry knocks on Mandy's door to wake her up. She chooses what to wear and gets herself ready. In the kitchen she makes a breakfast of cereal and tea and washes up.

On Tuesdays she walks to the top of the lane and meets the Camfields minibus. At the resource centre she checks with Shirley what the daily plan is and chooses what she wants to do. On returning home she listens to CDs or watches television in her room. June cooks the evening meal but Mandy helps by laying and clearing the table. In the evening she may go for a walk on her own or she may go to see Millie, a family friend. Sometimes she is asked out with June and Terry to see friends in the village. June goes with Mandy to help choose her clothes. She also advises on her hairstyle. Mandy has been offered two holidays this year. The resource centre is organising one in Wales and Cambridge Regional College is organising one in Norfolk. Mandy likes spending money on clothes which June gives to her.

Mandy

Mandy likes modern casual clothes with comfortable but smart shoes. She does not like frilly dresses, preferring jeans. Her favourite meal is Chinese followed by ice-cream. She likes meat but not fish and salads. Her CD collection is pop, disco, and Irish music, but nothing old-fashioned. Mandy loves trips with her family. Her ideal trip is to the beach. Mandy likes swimming and horse-riding. She is fond of animals. Benson, her new puppy, is well cared for. She likes drawing, painting and dancing. The discos at the riding school, the college and the centre are greatly enjoyed. Mandy would like to be more in charge of her life.

In Duxford, there are a number of people she likes, friends of the family. They pop round to see Millie. Peggy and her husband Ted visit. Mandy helps in the garden of Jane from nursery school. She likes Jane and her partner Steve. At Camfields, Mandy likes Susan who is nice and smiles a lot as well as Carol who goes to the college.

She gets on well with Richard and James. Very occasionally Mandy is involved in an argument but she can speak up for herself. Sometimes she gets upset and does not like people shouting. Shirley, her keyworker, is seen as a friend by Mandy who describes her as kind and helpful. Lynn Jenkins and Naomi Postlethwaite CPN (community nurse) are popular too. However no friends are ever been brought back home from Camfields. Apart from her family and their friends Mandy only meets other people with disabilities. She is warm and open and should easily make friends .

Mandy is skilled at horse-riding and swimming. Judith Walker, her tutor at the Cambridge College of Agriculture and Horticulture, is pleased with her progress. Mandy has completed the first section of NVQ level 1 in horse-riding and stable management. The arrangement of letters around the riding arena are now understood by Mandy, thus aiding her reading. She does some gardening at Bottisham Village College which she attends from Camfields on Thursday mornings. She is a skilled gardener trained by her father.

At Camfields she may do painting and simple sewing. The workshops concentrate on cutting film and assembling television plugs. On Thursday afternoons she may go with a group to the Abbey swimming pool. In the past Mandy worked well in the Camfields kitchen, clearing up and preparing salads using a knife.

At the Cambridge Regional College attended on Mondays, Tuesdays and Wednesdays, Mandy does cooking and arts and crafts. She uses a computer but is not making much headway. She is learning to read and write. She travels to the college alone on the bus. On Friday afternoons Mandy works at Newton Hall Little Hands Nursery playing with the children and clearing up. She did attend Snakehall Farm but didn't like it as it was too noisy. Mandy has many physical skills and can care for herself without help. At home she vacuums, dusts, tidies and polishes and cleans the bathroom. Terry's car is cleaned with the hose-pipe. She rides a bike and drives the tractor.

Mandy has had a number of disappointments in her life. She worked for over a year at the Ditton Walk nursery school without pay. After a time it became too noisy and was stopped. She worked for a term, half-day a week, doing Meals on Wheels without pay but she liked it. There was an offer of one day a week at The Red Cross charity shop in Burleigh St, Cambridge. She was turned away on her second visit in a disrespectful way. She was upset at the time. However Mandy is a very resilient person and got over this. She's still recovering from a broken romance that ended painfully.

She feels lonely and sad at times. She would like a friend of her own age without a disability. Later on she would like another boy friend. She has a lot of inner strength. She is a happy and very healthy woman with an excellent memory particularly for faces, events and people. Sometimes Mandy finds it hard to say what she thinks. At a Camfields meeting she spoke clearly about her ideas on incentive pay but afterwards got upset.

She has other fears – of storms, of people banging about around her, of too much traffic on the roads. At seven years old she was knocked down by a car. She may agree with suggestions in order to please. Sometimes when asked her first response is 'No'. This may be more about self-doubt than a lack of memory. If her parents are present she'll wait for them to answer, if alone she works it out. Naturally June and Terry struggle between their instinct to help and understanding that she has to work it out.

At present Mandy receives Severe Disablement Allowance and Income Support. There are two payments of £90 and £17.85p totalling £107.85p. She also receives an incentive payment from Camfields of £1.50p per week, as Mandy only attends one day a week this would come to 30p! However she is pleased to earn it. There is some concern by her parents at the price of her shoes. Mandy has problems with her feet.

Recommendations
- This plan could have direct funding possibilities, receiving cash and not services in kind. It would benefit Mandy to come out of the disability network and into the real community.
- Could we find a friend of her own age to go to discos and to share with? This woman could include Mandy into her own circle of friends. It would be useful if she owned a car.
- When Mandy is ready to leave home she would like to either:

    Share with one other person with a disability whom she liked

or
- Live with another person without a disability. (Lifeshare scheme.)
- Mandy would need support in her new home and encouragement to be more independent.
- Mandy would like to live near to her parents; they are considering moving from Duxford.
- Mandy is considering a job; some ideas are office work, cooking, or working in a café or nursery. Working with animals, particularly horses, is another idea. The main idea is of gardening. It would seem that somewhere quiet, with some variety, would be worth thinking about. A job coach, who would fade out, should be considered.
- We should investigate the present benefits. Is she getting the correct amount? She would like to collect benefits herself and learn about managing money. Her mother would like to help.
- Leaving Camfields and the Cambridge Regional College and doing a job would mean leaving behind friends. Mandy would still like to see Susan and Carol at times, perhaps for tea.
- Horse-riding should continue, perhaps the Sunday cross-country group. Also swimming, but exploring non-disabled groups.
- Work to continue on reading, writing, and numeracy. Counting and understanding of money are important. Perhaps support workers could assist on a one-to-one basis; explore the possibilities for community classes.
- More help is needed in computer work because she enjoys using them.
- A local drawing class might benefit her.
- Could someone help Mandy with simple sewing skills? She would like to make doll's clothes for Gemma.
- Mandy would like to improve her cooking. She would like to cook a meal for her parents.
- She would like to be less fearful in crossing roads.
- It is important that these changes are seen as being under her control.

Postscript

More recently I spoke to Mandy about making the plan, asking her what she remembered, particularly at the beginning. 'I thought it was good because we could talk and I could make us some tea.' The first meeting was at my home, how had that been? 'David asked me questions and made me laugh, my mum and dad wanted the care plan for me. We did not write anything down because Althea was making the tea. We all laughed a lot. We went for a walk to the pond.'

I reminded her about the second meeting at her home when I asked her some questions about when she was a child. Who had answered those questions? She replied that her father had, when I asked why, she said 'because I thought he knew better. We did not do much that time as it was hot and we sat under a tree in the garden'.

At the next meeting Mandy and I decided we wanted to be on our own. Mandy remembers: 'I went into the kitchen and made Althea a cup of tea. Then I answered her questions, we could check some questions with dad later.' At a later meeting I read some stuff back to Mandy and I'd got it wrong. Could Mandy recall how that had felt? 'It was a good feeling, we laughed at Althea getting it wrong. It wasn't nasty laughter, it was funny. It was nice for me to be right.'

The first idea that we had together was about finding a friend, Mandy remembers how pleased she was. I reminded her that she also wanted to work, but unsure in which sort of employment. So we had a lot of ideas to talk and think about and every week I reminded Mandy about this. 'This was a puzzle!' Mandy laughs,'My job and no one else's!' Another important thing had been cooking. 'I wanted to learn to cook my own dinner and make a meal for mum and dad.'

Our last meeting had been with mum and dad and we read them the plan. Terry was surprised at how much Mandy had remembered and only made a small correction, the name of the school. Mandy remembered how pleased they were. I asked about how she had felt. 'Good, yes, I did enjoy it. The best bit was talking about myself.'

One Year On
I talked with Mandy at home in Duxford about the changes since we last met. The care plan had influenced the agency organising her support. Mandy had left home and settled in a group home with two other people who had learning difficulties, opposite where her parents lived, closer to the city centre.

Our plan recommended that she should live with only one other person whom she liked. She'd had no opportunity to choose her fellow residents and was uncomfortable with them. The family agreed that she had been offered no alternatives. As her parents now worked for the organisation supporting their daughter, they were aware of the organisational difficulties. They felt that Mandy's care was insufficient and she needed to learn more skills.

Mandy was becoming unhappy and increasingly went across the road to her parents. Unfortunately this resulted in an accident. She was knocked down by a car and had to move back to live with her parents. It took her a long time to get over the accident and she's lost confidence in handling traffic.

Another important recommendation was for Mandy to get a job. She has paid work at the Little Hands nursery for two days a week. The rest of the week contains an educational session in environmental and social skills, numeracy, and budgeting at Sawston Village college. Another day is spent gaining an NVQ in waitressing at the Compass point tea-room in Sawston. There is a free day where she visits a local advocacy group called 'Speaking Up'. She also attends an innovative scheme 'Opportunities Unlimited'. This involves people with learning difficulties and others in work and leisure opportunities. She also attends an art, photography, and music course on Saturday afternoons.

Mandy still enjoys horse-riding and has been chosen to compete internationally by the Disabled Riders Association. Last year she won a gold and two bronze medals. She has her own computer and is developing more skills. Rollerblading and skiing are new pursuits and Mandy still loves swimming. She has improved her cooking but still needs help in timing meals and using hot surfaces.

Another recommendation was to find a friend of her own age without a disability. Her parents are looking into a YMCA scheme that offers dance and aerobic groups. A few months ago, Mandy talked of moving. An approach to the care planning agency has meant a new plan, which the parents are currently considering. They were impressed with the thorough and practical approach of the professional but the care plan was disappointing. The boxes on the complicated forms didn't fit Mandy.

I asked what the parents would like for their daughter. Mum responded: 'To be in her own home with one or two people without learning difficulties. Or with a person who had learning difficulties if she was really happy with her.' Mum felt that Mandy needed support in independent living skills. A support worker coming in for a couple of hours most evenings and at some time during the weekend would be sufficient. This arrangement could be flexible and gradually faded out and need not be expensive. Dad was concerned that she often seemed lonely and felt that two people around, coming and going, would be ideal.

They felt that direct funding arrangements would be good. I asked why. Mum said that there was a tendency for Mandy to copy inappropriate behaviour from other people with disabilities. She would be better outside the disability world. Dad felt that she was subject to pressures by being forced to live with other disabled people. She was sensitive and often worried about other residents. She was cast in a supporting role and unhappy with the responsibility.

I was pleased to learn that the essence of the original care plan was still important to them. Mandy had gained confidence during the process. Despite the shock of the accident, she still expresses her needs clearly. I hope that she and her parents will be listened to.

Themes
- struggle by parents to set their daughter free. Love can be so imprisoning especially after two car accidents. Mandy's life training had been to fit in with powerful others
- finding non-disabled friends when Mandy lives almost exclusively, when outside the family, in a world populated by people with disabilities
- desire to work and earn money. Need for a job coach?
- Mandy hurt by bigotry when volunteering in a shop
- leaving existing day services, where she was discontented, to set up her own individually funded support
- Mandy's wish to gain confidence and increased control over her own life.

Chapter 6
Kirsty

At seven, I was diagnosed with a progressive neuromuscular disorder never previously seen in women in the UK. When I was 18 I wanted to leave home. The second fact is not unusual. The first fact is and, no, 'progressive' in this case certainly does not mean new and exciting.

The question is: who am I? I am 23, Scottish (well, living in England but the child of two proper Scots), Labour supporting, pop music loving, shopaholic. I may not have a Scottish accent but I'm Scottish where it counts – i.e., I love whisky and I burn in the sun. I love shopping, particularly for clothes. I have problems with my hair. I am a firm believer in human rights and believe we live in an unjust society. I believe we are all responsible for each other and that able-bodied people should stick up for disabled people, that white people should endeavour to stamp out racism and that young people should protect the rights of older people.

I believe that 'The Whole of the Moon' was the best song ever written and I defy anyone to listen to Elgar's Cello Concerto played by Jacqueline Du Pré and not cry. I love really really crap pop music and I think that directors of large corporations are grossly overpaid. If I had a hero it would be Lois Keith.* I work four days a week in a Citizen Advocacy project for people with learning difficulties as I believe that people with learning difficulties are the people most discriminated against by our capitalist, sizest, perfectionist society. I'm vegetarian and I have a passion for spinach. Did I mention I used a wheelchair? Did I need to?

I began needing some assistance when I was about 13. At this point my parents approached my apparently free-thinking comprehensive school and asked if the timetable could be changed to involve fewer room changes and no stairs. They refused, and in the first of many battles I have come to expect at every corner, we persuaded the local education authority to pay for me to go to an independent boarding school. Bingo; at 14 I became mentally, personally, and spiritually independent, and lots of fantastic nuns who believed that all children were entitled to be educated together (without boys, naturally) got me through secondary and into Anglia Poly with three A levels and a slightly misguided view of catholicism.

I didn't come from the most usual of backgrounds. While all this was going on my father was developing a series of brain tumours and my stepmother was looking after everyone, so I had to go to college. Curiously this was later the reason for accessing the council house list – because I couldn't go home at the

* Lois Keith 'Mustn't Grumble' 1994 The Women's Press

end of my degree course I had to be housed, meaning conversely that, if I could have gone home, I would have been forced to do so and my life would not have turned out to be in my control.

When I started university there were two options for students with disabilities. One was to go to one without a specialist unit and organise personal assistants with dubious support from the welfare officers; the second was to go to a specialist unit. I chose Anglia, chiefly because of the specialist units in Cambridge. So I got Bridget's, a hostel for students with severe physical disabilities with 24-hour care, and Bridget's got me.

Life at Bridget's was somewhat haphazard for a number of reasons. Firstly, the unit opened with my intake and so there were teething problems. Secondly, the five students were completely mismatched as individuals. Our vastly different needs for assistance meant that the staffing was a perpetual nightmare – half of us were always unhappy. However, the experience did teach me a number of things – most importantly independence, skills for using personal assistance, and clear knowledge that I never ever wanted to share a house with anyone ever again. The security of the set-up was fantastic for the first year but became oppressive after that. I have a peculiar aversion to living by other people's rules!

During the last few months at Bridget's, I had to work towards organising some kind of future. I planned to take a year off before starting any serious job hunting to get things sorted out in the house and wanted to try voluntary work to see if I could work full time.

I wanted 24-hour care. I have difficulty using my upper body to do things such as eat, drink, wash, sit up unaided for more than a few minutes, and by then needed help with all the activities of daily living. I am also in quite a lot of pain. I need it to be absolutely fail safe as my fall-back positions are largely limited to various friends. My initial intention was to use Community Service Volunteers (CSV) to provide all the support. I would need two people to live in and provide support, including personal care tasks, driving, cleaning and housework, shopping. . . .

However, I discovered that for CSV to find a steady stream of women over 21 (for car insurance) who wanted to work with me in this area was almost impossible. I started to look at one CSV and a paid personal assistant, with the CSV enabling the paid carer to have breaks. At this point I also got a new local social worker (having previously been supported by one from my home town) who was fantastically dynamic and organised, able not only to listen but also to hear. She chose not to look for obstacles in the system but rather for ways to get round them. She put up all my curtain rails in her own time as well.

Kirsty

At this stage I didn't know that I wanted to plan my own care – at one stage I thought that was what everyone was doing. I knew clearly what I wanted and didn't want in a care package and with the social worker's help I began to go through the options. One of many things that impressed me was that she didn't at any point try to tell me what I did or did not need but constructively helped me to look at all the areas in which I might need help and how those needs might be met. There is something inherently infuriating about a health care professional of any background telling people with disabilities what they do or do not need. People tend to be misinformed and need informing but social workers asking people if they are sure they can't make a cup of tea, manage the toilet on their own, need a bath every day, should be a disciplinary offence.

I wanted someone to be there 24 hours a day. I wanted as few different people doing it as possible but as we looked into the options they looked increasingly expensive. It happened that just at this time a friend began working for a local agency called Christies Care, which specialised in live-in care at a fraction of the charges of other organisations. Hurrah! I entered into a contract with them to provide me with female personal assistants over 21 with a clean driving licence (if I had my way they'd be vegetarian and non-smoking), and they now try to fulfil it. However, at the time of writing there is only one regular personal assistant who fulfils all these criteria.

Christies has served me well over the last two and a half years. They were not previously known to my social worker but since I started using them the number of bookings in the area has multiplied rapidly. I've gone from being the youngest client by about 40 years to being one of several. They have supplied me with some excellent personal assistants (some have even returned!), some reasonable ones and a couple of diabolical ones. Worst case scenarios have included theft by personal assistants, walking out in the middle of the night, and verbal abuse. This is before we get to the perpetual problem of personal assistants misusing my orange badge. The drawback of an agency like this is that with all the will in the world they can't always know what their personal assistants are up to. I've found they respond to problems effectively in most cases. When a personal assistant gets ill, falls down the stairs, or whatever someone else has the problem of replacing them.

The good personal assistants tend to be the ones able to work under their own initiative and who take the time to listen to what it is I want them to do. There is nothing more wearing than having to check up on personal assistants: have they done the washing: put petrol in the car, remembered to get bread at Sainsburys?

Possibly equal to this in irritation are the personal assistants who constantly ask lots of personal questions or make comments about the house or my lifestyle. There is an ongoing fascination for some about my vegetarianism, ranging from the 'you can't be healthy' approach to the 'you'll never stick with it' notion (eight years and counting). Equally there are also discussions, without my approval, between personal assistants about my personal habits. There isn't really much I can do about it – except reduce the number of people I have contacts with in that role and who know that I'm obsessed with wearing the same colour bra as knickers, take zinc and oil of evening primrose supplements, and have a liking for Clinique toiletries.

My own experience is that personal assistants who are good at interpersonal skills and performing acts of personal care tend not to be so good at the housework and the practical side of things. Constant reminders work but this is tiring and energy consuming so sometimes I compromise and live in a mess. It is easy to ask why I don't try to get assistants who do both but this seems impossible most of the time. I have a network of friends with physical disabilities who use agencies and Christies is one of the best. It says something about the status of personal assistants in today's society that people who would well fulfil the role are unattracted by caring as the pay and conditions of service are often terrible.

I now work four days a week for a small local charity supporting choice for people with learning difficulties. On my fifth day I either have a break, do some freelance work as a trainer, or write. My disability has worsened so that I am now unable to walk, stand, transfer, lift my arms, wash, dry, or dress myself. The personal assistants drive me around in my adapted vehicle. I am lucky because of the range of specialist equipment helping my independence, including a powered wheelchair, powered mobile arm-support, and an electric bed. I also have a hoist which is the scourge of the equipment field. If the EU can spend millions making strict regulations about lifting and handling, they can make equipment that doesn't involve suspension from the ceiling.

I'm not sure that there is really a typical day in my life, but the work of the personal assistant usually remains consistent. Each morning I get up at a time arranged the night before. I'm not good in the mornings and if it is a new personal assistant I go though the routine the night before. When I wake up in the morning I am extremely tender all over and my body temperature tends to plummet as soon as the covers are removed. It is important for the assistant to work quickly and effectively to minimise the damage to my muscles likely at this time. Getting up and ready takes more than an hour if I'm washing my hair. After this I like to have breakfast and read the mail, then get to work.

My biggest gripe with all assistants is an inability to get things to happen on time. I am taken to work with everything I need whilst there. Daytime varies but chiefly the assistant is either at home doing housework and running errands or taking me wherever it is I need to be. When I get home, the assistant prepares dinner, clears up, and either drives me if I am going out or may help with something at home. She then enables me to go to bed and is on call overnight although this is rarely needed.

There are positive and negative things about using agencies for care. On the negative side, I don't know who is with me until they arrive each week. You have no real way of controlling who comes as this is largely dictated by the assistants. However, there is so much peace of mind having someone else organise them. I tend to have most success with young women of a similar background to myself travelling around the world. I have not been interested in employing my own care support as the administration and risks seemed too formidable. It is the most stressful aspect of my life but I still fervently believe that living independently is worth it.

Buying in and planning care are fraught with difficulty. I am currently looking at ways of employing my own personal assistants as legislation means that I am now considered trustworthy to spend money given for care; a moot time to remind the world that there is no one who has too much money for care. I hope to recruit for myself when Cambridge provides a back-up and support service, which hopefully involves a payroll aspect. The more time spent administering the assistants' salaries the less I have for working, living, and eating chocolate. I hope that small groups of people with similar needs will support each other in emergencies. However, I fear that my desire to pay people well and to give good working conditions will not be possible at current levels of funding. I am optimistic that there are people who would like to work in Cambridge for a year on their way round the world. Some might even want to work with me.

About a year ago, one regular personal assistant asked me if I really wanted her to stay another week as she had been tired and grumpy the week she'd been here. She suggested I might like a week off too. I reminded her – I never get a week off.

Themes
- greater individualising of services to meet Kirsty's particular needs
- more-effective payment system for personal assistants
- the continual battle against bureaucracy
- need for a support system for those employing assistants, which provides, for example, payroll services
- facilitation skills of a good social worker.

Chapter 7
Joan

Lana Morris

Following a meeting with a statutory housing organisation which provides general, sheltered, and very sheltered housing, I received a referral from the unit manager. I was asked to devise a care plan for Joan as staff were becoming increasingly concerned. They felt she was 'difficult' and would be a 'challenge' for me. Joan was known as someone who 'yelled at staff' and, since moving to the unit, had lost skills in walking. She was also seen as 'depressed and frustrated with herself'. Staff hoped that a care plan would highlight current needs to help staff find alternatives and ways to support her.

I arranged a meeting with Joan and we discussed doing a care plan. She agreed to be involved, although felt she was an uninteresting person. The following is Joan's care plan and recommendations. It was based upon the four magnets – devised by Brandon and Brandon (1993) and further covered in Atherton and Brandon (1996).

Care Plan
Joan is a warm, friendly, 80-year-old, with greying hair and of medium height. She was born in Liverpool and has a great sense of humour, which is often hidden by sadness.

Joan was an only child and lived with her parents until her late teens. Her father died while she was quite young. She enjoyed travelling around the country and visited America and Spain. She worked as a production assistant on aircraft parts. She met her husband late in life and, after marrying, moved to the local area and has lived here for the last 30 years. Her husband had been previously married and had two children; he and Joan chose not to have children. He died in 1982.

Joan moved into very sheltered accommodation in 1995, following a stroke and fall in 1990. Since the stroke, Joan is less able to walk and now uses a wheelchair to get around. There are seven people in this section, each in a separate flat. Meals are communal in the residents' kitchen/dining room.

Control
Joan has little control in her life. Her days are dictated by the staff shifts. Joan wakes up between 6 and 7a.m., although since taking sleeping tablets she finds it more difficult to awake. Staff come in at 7.30a.m., get her out of bed, tend to

her personal care, and help her dress. 'Usually they ask me what I want to wear, but I say, oh, just anything because I know they haven't got much time to be with me, so I don't want to make them have to stay longer.' She has a daily shower and once weekly is taken downstairs for a bath. Staff try to offer choices to stay in bed longer if she wants and to choose clothes.

After dressing, Joan is taken to the dining room opposite. She has breakfast, usually toast and marmalade. 'I can do this myself. That's about all I can do.' Once breakfast is over, she is returned to the flat where she watches television. Staff come at 11a.m. with tea or coffee. Joan has tea-making facilities but since the stroke and the need for the wheelchair she can no longer make drinks and has to rely on staff.

At lunch-time, staff take her to the dining room and return her after the meal. She then watches television and sometimes has a sleep. Joan likes watching documentaries and talk shows. 'I don't like the Australian soaps and I've gone off Coronation Street.'

The same ritual occurs at tea-time and between 8 and 9 p.m. Joan goes to bed. 'I'm tired and bored by then.' Staff assist her in getting ready. This is Joan's typical day. She sees herself as boring others. 'I would like to help them [staff]. I do like them, they are good but it isn't the same as doing things for yourself. I try to content myself, but I know it's quicker for staff to do it themselves. It can be really frustrating. I want to try to do things but I'm scared of trying in case I can't do it or take up too much of their time.'

Joan has no control over her finances. Rent and bills are paid by direct debit and staff collect her benefits. However, this is changing and, in future, benefits will be paid directly into Joan's bank account. If she wants money from the bank, she asks staff to collect it and sometimes goes with them. The last time she remembers going out was for Christmas shopping. However, staff say she has been shopping at the Grafton centre and on occasions shopped in the high street since then.

Laundry is collected twice a week by staff. Housework is done by staff as is some personal care. Twice weekly Joan's friend visits and dusts.

Skills
Joan had a skilled job in the aircraft industry. Since the stroke she has been less able to do the things she likes. She was a keen cook and used to make cakes for her husband. She enjoyed the garden and planting. She also enjoys reading but needs large print. Due to a right-sided weakness in her body, she is no longer able to hold a book and turn pages. She doesn't like talking tapes or videos.

Joan

She loves the opportunity to go into the town centre, look at clothes and enjoy the 'busy, bustling' at the market. She has little opportunity to do this, because of staff shortages.

Joan would love to help in the kitchens, either preparing meals or just being around, watching what people do. 'I prefer my own cooking but can't do that any more. I'd like to help cook but they haven't got time for me and I probably wouldn't be allowed in the kitchen. Since the chef left the food is not as good. It's so monotonous sometimes. I especially hate the blancmange.'

Joan feels useless and battles with the loss of skills. 'My walking is better than of late but I feel unsteady and need someone around me. For a time I would try and walk around my flat on my own but I find this too difficult now. I use my wheelchair but it isn't very comfortable. I'd like to get a better one.' Staff assist Joan in walking to the bathroom in her flat. She has an alarm cord to call for assistance. 'They tell me they'll only be a minute but take ages to come. I know they are busy but I only ring when I really want them. I try not to take up too much of their time. It does annoy me when they are longer than they say they'll be.'

Joan enjoys buying things and says that, although being an impulse buyer, she has an eye for a good bargain. She would enjoy doing something in the day.

Joan has such a wonderful sense of humour and communicates so well. She tries hard not to be a bother or to focus on her problems. Instead she likes to find out what you do, what you enjoy, and what places you've visited. She is a good listener and enjoys having a laugh which sadly is rare these days.

Pain

Joan has seen a lot of pain, a lot from the war years. Physically she has 'lost my old self' since the stroke and found it difficult to become dependent on others. 'I used to do so much myself. I'm lucky because I've had a nice life and I didn't expect to last to be this age but I'm not the woman I used to be. I am a different person and sometimes I don't like me.' She gets depressed, due to so little happening in her life, and exhausted from the physical effort she has to make since the stroke. She often feels hopeless.

She is in frequent physical pain. Her arm is sore and stiff and is frustrated that she can't do anything with it. She attends physio which has eased the pain a little. She also feels pain when staff try to assist. 'The staff are unaware that sometimes they hurt me. It's unintentional but they often go to my right side to get me up and my arm is in so much pain – they need to know which arm I use. In general they're good and I like living here.'

Joan takes the following medication:–

Amytriptyline	–	To help sleep and calm
Aspirin dispersible	–	Heart
Bendrofluazide	–	Water tablet
Omeprazole	–	Hiatus hernia
Becbnethasone	–	Asthma
Salbutamol inhaler	–	Asthma.

She worries about lost skills. When she first arrived at the unit she could use a zimmer frame. She sometimes gets confused and this upsets her. She hates the boredom and ' . . . takes it out on staff. Like this morning this staff member came in and I really felt like tormenting her. It was only about something small but I really wanted to torment her today. Then I said to myself that I was really cruel and didn't used to be like this. I felt really bad and I often wonder what they [staff] think of me.'

Joan worries about what staff think of her and taking up their time. She tries desperately hard to be 'no trouble' and gets upset when she has 'bad feelings' towards staff. She is seen by staff as being very depressed and frustrated and this seems to have gone on for a long time. Joan spends much time thinking about her husband and talks about how deeply she misses him. She often refers to him in the present tense. She doesn't talk very much about the stepchildren. 'They really don't care about me. It's a bit hurtful but I don't let it bother me now. They had most things from my old flat. It doesn't cause me pain any more. My stepdaughter has two girls. I don't bother with them now. The youngest granddaughter was lovely and used to visit. I'm nothing to them now. They were all grown up when I married my husband.'

She talks about giving up life. 'I've got no hope now. I don't care any more and I don't know what would make me care. I'm not bothering any more. I don't worry about dying. I wouldn't care if I went tomorrow. I've gone downhill since the stroke and my husband dying. I've not got a lot to look forward to. If I could go out or sit in the garden as the weather is better. I wish something would happen to me so I can just get out of the way.'

Contact
Joan has little contact with others, although staff see her as lucky as she has two friends who come to visit. A cousin keeps in contact and a neighbour comes to read to her. This is a lot more than some residents.

Joan

Joan's friend Louise comes, does dusting, makes tea, and has a chat. She is about the same age so can't offer to take her out. Her other friend also pops in regularly to see how she is and occasionally fetches some shopping.

Joan's neighbour used to come regularly to read and chat. 'He is a young man, probably in his 20s and I think he has problems too but I don't like to ask in case he thinks I'm nosey. He hasn't been around lately. I don't mind if he's fed up with me but I'm worried in case something has happened.'

Joan has a cousin who lives in the West Country who comes down for a week every year. Staff think this may be Joan's niece. Unfortunately she had to cancel the last visit due to her son having measles. Joan hopes they will be in contact again soon.

Most of Joan's contact comes through paid staff who can only attend to personal care and meals. Due to the rota, there is no time for them to have a chat or cup of tea. When they have time they try to arrange events like shopping.

There are social occasions held on the ground floor during evenings but Joan is nervous of joining in. People tend to talk about their various ailments. She worries about getting to and from her flat on time for these events and whether other residents will accept her. She worries about her image and feels she's scruffy in comparison with some other residents.

Recommendations

- Joan wants more control in her life like choosing clothes. Staff need to reassure Joan that she has time to make choices.
- She wants company. Someone who really wants to be with her and have a cup of tea or go out. Staff need to look for a volunteer. Perhaps CONTACT agency (a volunteer service, where students from the local university offer time) could help. This could be important in terms of support due to staffing levels. The volunteer would assist with some of her personal care when going out.
- Joan wants to go with staff in collecting benefits or going to the bank. She likes to go out and has little opportunity at present.
- Joan enjoys cooking and gardening. Could she spend some time in the kitchens, helping prepare lunches? What about a cookery course? Can she help in the garden or plant window boxes? It has been mentioned that the unit may look at providing a cookery session for the residents. The advantage for Joan might be that she gets to know some residents better and feels more comfortable. A disadvantage is that she doesn't go out into the local community.

- Staff need to look at transport, particularly if she joins an afternoon or evening class outside. Is she eligible for the voluntary drivers scheme? What about the taxi service? Has she been assessed for mobility allowance? Could a volunteer be a driver?

- Joan would like a more comfortable wheelchair. Staff could get information on various wheelchairs and invite sales reps to meet Joan and/or for her to visit organisations to choose the most comfortable chair. Could the physiotherapy department help?

- She wants opportunities during the day to help alleviate her loneliness and depression. She is nervous of meeting people at social events. Could staff accompany and help her to feel more acceptable?

- Joan feels the loss of her 'old' self. She has lost confidence and some motivation. She needs opportunities to talk about how she feels and what would help. Perhaps her GP could offer or put her in touch with counselling.

- Joan enjoys being read to and would also like to read herself. When was the last time she had a sight test? This should be done with staff assistance and help Joan to find aids/adaptations that can hold a large-print book so she can use her left hand to turn the pages.

- Once in a while Joan would like to have her hair and make-up done. Staff could help Joan make a hairdressing appointment. Perhaps this could be done prior to visits out, i.e. morning at the hairdressers, shopping in the afternoon.

- Staff should know that Joan prefers to get out of bed with assistance from the left. She mentions that staff occasionally cause her pain due to helping her from the right. Her right arm is particularly sore since the stroke.

- Joan wants involvement in implementing the care plan. Perhaps she can have access to the staff office to make phone calls regarding classes and other opportunities, or to contact her friends or relatives. She'll need staff assistance and support.

- Joan needs valuing and the opportunity to enjoy life and share joys and sorrows. Staff should encourage and support her in attending outings, events, meeting people as well as respecting her solitude. She needs listening to.

Process

Mutually agreed meetings were arranged every week for about one hour at a time. There were seven in all. The first consisted in explaining the purpose of the care planning and that we would come up with a document detailing her current situation and compiling a list of recommendations, based on discussions and notes from each meeting. Each week I'd write up the meeting and return to Joan to read through and highlight any errors, make changes or query what had been written. In this way, Joan controlled the document and could check that I got things right and was really listening.

The first meeting took place in her flat. I was with a student from Kiev and we introduced ourselves. I explained why we were there; to try to work together on producing a care plan to try to find options which might improve her daily life. I checked that Joan was happy with this. She was glad to meet us but felt confused about why there was suddenly so much attention. I explained that the unit manager referred her because staff were concerned about her depression. I asked her if she was happy to go ahead. She wanted to continue but said she wasn't an interesting person.

We spent an hour getting to know each other, finding out some of her interests and background. Joan said a couple of times, 'I don't know where to start. I'm not very interesting really.' I asked about where she'd lived before moving here and Joan began telling us about the past. She had difficulty remembering dates but gave a bitter-sweet picture of life. She often mentioned her husband. 'I missed him dreadfully when he died. I still do.' She had been fairly happy until the stroke which left her right side partially paralysed. This had a major impact on her and she talked of feeling 'useless', 'uninteresting' and 'a different person than I used to be'. Her days were dull and boring, depressing and exhausting due to the physical effort necessary since the stroke. It was a difficult meeting as she had little energy and said a couple of times: 'I don't really want anything. I can't do anything.' We chatted for a while about working on aircraft and some foreign holidays. We arranged to meet the following week to look at issues of control.

The following meeting was in Joan's flat. The TV was on and she seemed angry. She was startled when I knocked on the sitting-room door and told me to come and sit down. We sat in silence for a few minutes then she said that 'they' hadn't left the morning paper and where were 'they'? I asked if she wanted me to find one of 'them' and see about the paper but she brushed this aside. After a few minutes of uncomfortable silence, I explained about writing up the notes from last week. Did she want to check that I'd got things right. She read them through and at the end said they were fine. I asked if she wanted to carry on by looking at how much control she had, starting with what her usual day is like. Her general feeling was that she has little control and that staff didn't really want to be around her. She sometimes felt like tormenting staff. I commented that I couldn't really visualise her at 5ft 2ins wielding a wheelchair menacingly. We both laughed and it was the first time I'd seen her laugh. She said it made her feel so frustrated being unable to do things. She knew it was quicker for staff to do things, it left her feeling scared to try in case she was incapable.

We went on to list things that she'd like to do. She stressed that staff were doing their best and because she is a Liverpudlian, she was used to criticising. Down here staff take it all so personally! She was anxious about meeting other residents.

On my third visit I found Joan alone in the dining-room. She explained that staff were late in starting and she'd also slept late. She asked me to take her into the flat so we could talk. She was very wheezy and chesty and looked tired but seemed cheerful. She read through the notes, commenting that she hadn't realised we'd talked so much last time. She mentioned about going to the physio for a check-up in six weeks' time.

Joan said that recently she'd felt much better and that walking had improved a little. She'd tried walking in her flat but hadn't told staff this. She didn't mind using a wheelchair but would like a better one. She had gone off food in recent weeks but felt the appetite was returning. She talked of the joy of gardening, cooking, and other interests. She felt 'in a state of limbo – I'm a patient woman, I have to be. It's no use being anything else'. She aimed to keep going but missed Liverpudlian humour. 'There was always a lot of banter, I always talked a lot.' She was beginning to feel better and might go downstairs to meet some other residents. We looked at what skills/hobbies she'd like to go back to as well as developing new ones and where to get information.

On our fourth meeting Joan was looking out of the window and the TV was on loudly. She said she felt very down. She had a quiet Easter and was disappointed that her friend was unable to visit and that her niece and baby couldn't come because the child had chickenpox. She read through last week's notes and didn't have much to say. I asked if she wanted to leave the care plan and just sit and talk. She talked about the staff's comings and goings and then about when she first moved in. She talked about the loss of her husband, the lack of contact with his children, and loss of skills and confidence. Joan's energy was very low. She was disappointed that Easter had turned out less promising and was fed up with the unit. She wanted to go out but it was too cold and wet. We looked at the available options and where to get information on activities, wheelchairs, going shopping, and volunteers.

My next visit looked at the draft care plan. Joan read it all through and agreed with it. I proposed we met with the unit leader to discuss implementation. Joan did not want to meet with the unit leader. She felt that this might be seen as her causing 'trouble' and that things were all right really. It would be better that I met with the unit manager alone.

The manager of the unit was a very pleasant woman with an air of world weariness. I discussed the meetings with Joan and went through the draft care plan with her. I voiced concern over the isolation Joan was in. The manager responded defensively that Joan had two friends visiting and this was much more than other residents. She acknowledged that Joan seemed depressed but when I asked whether the GP had been contacted about a referral for counselling, she said no one wanted to upset the GP further. The GP was unhappy as someone had done a care plan a few weeks previously and contacted him with regard to medication. The GP had taken offence and felt his authority was being questioned. The unit manager didn't want to further undermine a good relationship.

As we went through the plan, the manager stressed that Joan had been out twice since Christmas, once to go shopping and once to the bank with staff. She had also had a sight test earlier in the year. Staff felt she was a selective reader. I thought she meant that Joan stuck to a particular style of author or preferred crime novels to romance but this wasn't the case. Staff meant that she said she needed large print but reads the newspaper so obviously her eyesight was not as poor as she'd have you believe! The manager said that of course they'd like to do more with the residents but with so many in the unit and so few staff not much could happen.

My next visit was great. She was really cheerful and relaxed and her hair had been done. That afternoon she was visiting the physio to see about her arm. I summarised the discussion with the manager and expressed regret that it was not as positive as I'd hoped. I gave Joan a list of the agencies I'd phoned for information and copied this to the unit manager. Joan and I laughed over something on TV and the air was warmer outside. She looked forward to her friend visiting later that morning and sitting in the garden. We talked at length about joining some in-house activities and how she'd felt about the process of the care plan. I arranged to visit the following week for the last time and hand over the care plan to the unit manager.

Joan's Comments

My final visit to Joan was spent looking in more detail at the process and how she'd felt about the last several weeks.

Joan made it clear that she felt much better in herself and this was because we'd looked at some things where some changes could take place. She was concerned about staff perceptions and was quick to say that they were nice and very busy, so she didn't expect too much. She'd enjoyed the weekly visits and going over materials from the previous discussion. Joan said, 'I've liked having someone to visit and talk, not just about me but also what's happening around, on the news and television and what things I could try if I wanted.'

In contrast, staff didn't feel the care plan process was successful. When discussing publishing the care plan, Joan was happy. However, the unit manager didn't want anything published as it didn't portray a positive picture for the staff and they'd be upset. As this was Joan's care plan, I suggested this was a good opportunity for staff to discuss how they perceived the situation but this was not received well. As far as staff were concerned, they were busy with the practicalities of caring for a number of people dependent on them. There was no time for further discussion.

This highlighted a difficult position. Joan has valid criticisms and concerns regarding her care, yet has to maintain the *status quo*. She is uncomfortable at discussing concerns out of worry about staff perceptions. Baker (1996) comments: 'The only way house bound and frail elderly people can usually contribute or comment is through the person actually supplying the services – something they're often more reluctant to do.'

She is seen by professionals as someone difficult to support and needs some change to alter the current situation. Wilson (1996) comments: 'The view that professionals know best and that non-compliance is the fault of the perverse user is no longer tenable, if it ever was. Time and trust are probably the key ingredients in a good outcome. Once again, these depend on workload, management and the support of front line staff.'

It would be easy to collude with staff by not publishing the material. They have a vested interest in assuring the outside world that things are running smoothly and that residents are happy, with all needs met. At the same time they acknowledge that, for some residents, including Joan, this isn't the real picture and aim to make changes but not too publicly. Marshall and Dixon note this tension between block provision and the individual needs. 'Bulk provision is always likely to ignore individual needs.' They analyse professional's views on older people and how they fit readily into ageist stereotypes. Often social workers have contact with older people in crisis. '... if this is the only experience workers have, it can be possible to develop a view that old age is in the most part about disabling and difficult times'. (Marshall and Dixon 1996)

Joan is in the centre of the process and it is her care plan to do with what she wants. She was happy to have it published to show how it should be done. Issues of consent to publish leave professionals very uncomfortable. Adams (1996) makes two points. The outcomes of challenges that service users make to professionals are difficult to predict. Secondly, workers enjoy their status and superiority and if they are insecure about professional credibility, there may be conflict between a keenness to see others develop skills yet '... reluctance to hand over to them responsibility and authority, and anxiety that non-professionals, however unwittingly, will do damage'. Perhaps professionals felt that publication might damage professional credibility because of the image of staff in the care plan.

The last part was handing over the plan to Joan and the unit manager. While the manager was positive about implementing some recommendations, she stressed that any action would take time. Joan was happy to wait, after all '... the staff were doing their best'.

Themes
- seeing Joan as autonomous person, avoiding a sophisticated and even benevolent oppression. Staff are unfamiliar with ideas of empowerment so she has little chance to make the major decisions in her life
- the service is concerned with its purposes and problems, not with the outcomes for Joan. The major element is to avoid bothering senior people with perceived high status like the doctor. Criticism is viewed as troublemaking
- staff see their work mainly in delivering meals and keeping things clean rather than in chatting to the residents so this contributes to Joan feeling lonely much of the time
- Joan suffers from the failure to develop a diffusive service, one which reaches out to the outside world. She needs to use some outside services – to go shopping, attend interesting events ...
- Increasingly she loses contact with friends.

References:

Adams, R. (1996) *Social Work and Empowerment*. Macmillan Press Ltd. Hampshire (2nd Ed).

Atherton, K.; Brandon, D. and Brandon A. (1996) *Handbook of Care Planning*. Positive Publications. London.

Baker, J (1996) 'Volunteer Partners give a voice to the frail elderly' *Care Plan*. Vol 3, No 1, Sept, pp27-9.

Brandon, D. and Brandon, A. (1994) *The Yin and Yang of Care Planning*. Anglia Polytechnic University. Cambridge.

Marshall, M., Dixon, M. (1996) *Social Work with Older People*. Macmillan Press Ltd. Hampshire (3rd Ed).

Wilson, G. (1996) 'Quality through Co-Production' *Care Plan,* Vol 3, No 1, pp13-5.

Chapter 8
Kavin

Graham Smith

Kavin is 40 years old, one of two children – both male. He was born in Wyke Regis near Weymouth in Dorset. He is a very large man with short hair flecked with grey. He has ruddy cheeks and dark brown eyes which dart about during conversation. His speaks openly about his life with a rich sense of humour. He talks of his service in the military. He served as a trooper in the Blues and Royals of the Queens Household Cavalry. Although he always sits in a wheelchair with one leg stretched straight out he is obviously a very big man.

He rents a flat, adapted to his physical disabilities, in Cambridge from Granta Housing Association. He moved in some six years ago after 11 years in Addenbrookes Hospital. Kavin likes to watch sport on TV, particularly Rugby Union. His favourite music is rock 'n' roll. He also listens to Newstalk on the tape recorder to keep in touch with current affairs.

He uses his wheelchair to get around the flat and also in Headway, visited on Tuesdays and Fridays. His parents live about 15 miles away and try to come two or three times a week, taking him in an adapted car to Headway, Dial-a-Ride doing the return journey. His mother does the shopping and washing. Kavin's brother lives in Haverhill and occasionally meets him at their parents' house on Sundays.

Control
Kavin feels in control over much of his life but would prefer more. He makes the choices over meals. Although he doesn't cook or prepare the food, he chooses what goes on the shopping list. He has a vacuum flask filled with hot or cold drinks, serving him throughout the day when thirsty. He enjoys black coffee. He goes on Sundays to roast lunch with his parents.

He controls his entertainment at home, operating the TV, radio, and hi-fi from a remote control switch. He listens to heavy metal music, especially AC-DC, Meatloaf, and old favourites Pink Floyd and Jefferson Airplane. He likes to watch TV – business and news programmes as well as sport and quiz games. He chooses the clothes from his wardrobe. His favourite colour is red.

He has control over the entry system to his flat, operated through a remote control switch. The door can be opened by key as well and Granta have a spare set.

He tries to spend time daily lifting weights to strengthen his arms and shoulders. He uses a Bullworker and dumb-bells.

He enjoys using a computer at Headway. He writes letters as well as keeping a journal. He enjoys pottery, using the gymnasium, listening to various seminars. It gives him a chance to socialise. He also goes on outings, some organised by Headway. His last holiday was two years ago, when he went to Chigwell in Essex.

Kavin has some physical movement in both arms. His grip is stronger in his left hand, which he prefers to use. He is described as paraplegic but has movement in both hands and arms.

Kavin would like more control over his finances and how the money is spent. He feels that the new Direct Payments system will give him more control and choice.

Skills
Kavin has many skills. He communicates extremely well being highly articulate with an extensive vocabulary. Before his head injury he had learnt sub-aqua diving, played as a prop forward for the Cheshire Rugby Union team, flown with the Air Training Corps, and received a Duke of Edinburgh bronze medal. He worked hard to get two parts of a City and Guilds radio and TV engineering/repairs award but then was made redundant. He learnt equestrian skills in the Army.

Since his head injury he has worked hard to relearn some skills to improve his quality of life. At Headway he uses a speech computer (ACORN) with an expanded keyboard that allows him to hear each letter or word entered. The words are magnified so he can read them before moving on. The font needs to be 48 or more for him to read it.

Kavin can do some personal care. He can wash and brush his teeth and empty his catheter. He makes toast in the mornings for breakfast. He helps himself to hot coffee of cold drinks from a flask filled by his carer. He can operate some electric gadgets by remote control – the electric door control, TV, phone, cassette deck, video monitor. . . .

He manages the small amount of money paid directly from Income Support. He has a bank account in his own name with a cheque-book.

Pain
He has had a great deal of pain in his life, both physically and emotionally. Whilst serving in the Household Cavalry, he was attacked by another trooper. They had been rehearsing a passing-out parade in full ceremonial kit, on

horseback. The horses shied suddenly and a trooper was thrown from his horse and blamed Kavin, who apologised. Later in the changing room, the trooper picked up a heavy wooden jackboot last and hit him over the head.

'There was a lot of blood and I was confused. I ended up in the medical centre.'

He spent two days in St George's Hospital and on release was questioned about the incident. The trooper who assaulted him was dishonourably discharged.

Through his injuries Kavin was given 14 days' leave to recover. He started to get blackouts but these eventually stopped. The rest of the troop blamed Kavin for the dismissal of their comrade and made life hell for him. By the time he left the cavalry 'I couldn't have cared less what happened to me'.

Later, when living in Brixton, he was again attacked but this time on the street. Someone leapt out at him, stabbing him several times in the stomach and the neck. 'My abdomen was like bits of spaghetti before rinsing. I started vomiting and bringing up blood so I went to hospital and they sorted me out and rebuilt my gut.'

Over a year later, he was suffering acute pain due to the swelling of both legs and his left arm, due to infected thrombosis. The leg, previously broken, was very swollen. His doctor prescribed palfium, a morphine derivative which made him feel 'disorientated and confused'. He accidentally overdosed, going into a coma for about 16 weeks. 'One night when I was in extreme pain I accidentally took an overdose of painkillers. I went into a coma and my mother found me and rang the doctor who got me rushed into hospital.' He spent about two weeks on a ventilator in Addenbrookes Hospital.

He came round from the coma and got physiotherapy twice daily. 'I was completely paralysed from the neck downwards. My left arm was the first thing to start moving.'

Kavin spent 11 years in Addenbrookes. He tried out several residential homes but none were suitable for his needs. This period brought him much anger and pain. His indomitable spirit and sardonic humour helped him to survive.

Currently he gets medication for pain

- Baclofen (anti-spasmodic tablet and muscle relaxant) 30 mgs 4x daily
- Diazepam (sleeping tablet) 5 mgs daily
- Paracetamol (headaches) when required.

He has no side-effects from this medication. He gets some pain from occasional pressure sores and from his back in the mornings. He is not sure why he doesn't get any physiotherapy.

His health is good. He has a good relationship with the District Nurse. Support also comes from the flexicare nursing service so he is seen regularly by both. He has been diagnosed by Barbara Wilson, a senior clinical neuro-psychologist, as having Balint's syndrome. This is a rare condition involving difficulty in locating objects spatially.

Contact

He has a close relationship with Mel, his girlfriend. She lives about two miles away and they keep in contact throughout the week.

His relationship with his parents is rather strained at present. They strongly object to him seeking further independence through direct funding. They wanted him to go into a Leonard Cheshire home where he could be well looked after and live in a safe and secure environment. His parents do not want to get involved in his future although they still provide some support.

During the last six years Kavin has received support from Granta Housing Association. He is generally content with the relationships developed although there have been some strains.

He has attended Headway for some years and generally gets on with people there. He is careful whom he chooses as friends but mentions David, John, and Ed. 'I don't make close friends easily. I keep my own counsel because the more I reveal the less people may believe me.' Given his rich and varied life, this is easy to understand.

Kavin also goes to the Meadows Community Centre in the Arbury. He does craft work and recently made a mobile sculpture. He attends a photographic group, which has awakened an old interest.

Recommendations
Direct Funding

Kavin is keen to go forward with direct funding, giving him his own money to spend on support and wants to see the video tape made by the government on direct funding as soon as possible. He desires to remain living in his Granta flat. The whole purpose of these fresh arrangements is to give Kavin *control over his life*. This means that those who will be supporting him fully understand that he needs to make the decisions about how he chooses to live. The support workers role is advisory.

Night Covers
Care call/Lifeline – Emergency night cover.
Kavin has been informed by Lifeline that he can continue with this service at a cost of £2.15 per week. However, he will need three named key-holders who can be contacted in an emergency. Granta representatives said that Kavin had used this service approximately three to four times since living in the flat. He has asked two people if they would be key-holders and they've agreed. They are Glynis Seymour and Andy Woodrow, both working for Granta. Lifeline needs to know about any change-over of key-holders – names, telephone numbers of new holders, etc.

Staff Training
When Kavin has appointed new assistants they require a two-hour training programme run by Chiltern Medical Development, the makers of the Wispa ceiling-mounted hoist and slings. This would cost approximately £50 for a group. Granta have offered to supervise before the actual change-over.

Appointing New Assistants
Kavin would prefer mainly to employ fresh people. He would ask a present assistant, who currently works for an agency, if he could work week-ends. He would seek new workers, advertising in newspapers, shops, community centres, libraries, etc. Kavin is looking for females – about 30 years old, articulate, and with knowledge of computers. They need to be physically strong and approximately 5 ft 10 ins plus.

There are many ways of employing people, on a full-time basis which means being responsible for the payment of wages, National Insurance contributions, and income tax. Kavin could employ people part time, provided they did not earn more than £62 per week, then there is no need to pay National Insurance contributions or income tax. Assistants could also be self-employed, responsible for their own sickness and holiday contributions.

Discussion with Kavin about his views on the current support routine and the need to involve his new assistants in devising a new routine. i.e., if he wanted to get up later, have his meals at different times. Staff should be clear on what his needs are. This should be written into a staffing contract. We are still not entirely clear on staffing levels. It would be beneficial for Kavin to have part-time staff rather than be dependent upon full-time, as this could cause problems if the full-time member went off sick or on holiday.

Aids/Adaptations
Kavin uses a hoist-and-sling arranged by social services. We are not clear about the service contract for maintenance and/or renewal. The present sling is the

most up to date on the market. Presently, Kavin sleeps in one sling which he finds unsatisfactory. We need to look at alternatives which Chiltern can help with.

Transport
Kavin presently relies on his father and Dial-a-Ride to take him where he wants to go. His father will continue to transport him in the foreseeable future. His weekly journeys are to Headway House on Mill Road in Cambridge. Every Tuesday and Friday Kavin makes the return journey, approximately 1.2 miles each way. Presently, his father takes him on both days, with Dial-a-Ride doing the return journey for £1. They need six days advanced notice before picking up Kavin.

His father has a Ford Escort Elite, adapted to suit Kavin's needs. The vehicle belongs to Kavin's father, who paid for it. The Motability scheme has not been used. The vehicle is registered in Kavin's name so that he can claim exemption from Vehicle Excise Duty. If Kavin wishes to look at alternative means of transport, he could use the Motability scheme.

1. Kavin buys a vehicle through a hire-purchase scheme arranged by the Motability scheme, provided the vehicle passes an AA inspection.

2. His father retains the vehicle and Kavin purchases a new vehicle through a 'Contract-Hire Scheme' arranged through Motability. This purchase could come through the mobility allowance. Details from various car dealers are available as is further information on the Motability scheme in the information pack compiled for Kavin. If you buy a vehicle on contract hire that has to be adapted, the cost increases twofold with the adaptations. Motability only covers the cost of the actual vehicle so, in order for the vehicle to be adapted, Kavin would need to either pay for these adaptations or apply for a grant through the Motability charitable fund. Kavin is severely disabled and can apply for a grant through the government mobility equipment fund. There is a current waiting time of approximately 18 months so he would need to apply shortly.

Computer/educational
Kavin prefers information on audio or video tape (preferably audio). He would like a computer at home. This would allow the running of software packages to assist him with accounting and further educational needs. Information about the computer comes from Headway and from the manufacturers to what best suits Kavin's needs. Suitable software is Dragon Dictate Solo, retailing at about £80. It is voice activated so requires no keyboard skills.

Kavin

Kavin is interested in further study and would like an Open University course – a BSc in disability studies. He needs information on relevant courses and about the possibility of getting a scholarship to assist with purchase of books and materials and towards the cost of the computer. He is eligible for a local authority grant.

Headway
Kavin attends two days a week and is happy with this. Sometimes he will use Dial-a-Ride for both journeys rather than relying on his father. Day trips may be arranged later in the year.

Health
New staff can get repeat prescriptions. Kavin needs regular information about side-effects and use of the medication.

Housing
The city council housing department has agreed that Kavin can take over the tenancy of the flat, provided he has an appropriate support package. In the future there could be other housing options. Kavin needs relevant documents relating to service contracts for the Wispa hoist-and-sling system, and the electronically operated door. All were arranged by social services and he needs to ensure this equipment is maintained.

Kavin should take out household and contents insurance and discuss with Granta what equipment he wants and what the cost is. The electrical appliances are about five years old and owned by Granta. The insurance policy is in his name but needs transferring so that he can take over payments. Granta have to decide whether to write off the cost of the equipment or sell it to Kavin. He has now taken over the tenancy of the flat with insurance for the contents.

Benefits/Bills
He needs his benefits checking to make sure he is gaining his full entitlements. He would also need a new bank account for any Direct Payments scheme.

All Kavin's benefits go directly to Granta with the exception of mobility allowance. He currently receives £299.10 per week on preserved rights (Income Support). The cost of the package of care from Granta is £285.00 per week, including the rent. This leaves £14.10 per week personal allowance. So far no claim has been made for Housing Benefit.

Kavin will not pay any Council Tax if he claims both Housing Benefit and Income Support. We are awaiting confirmation. Under a new tenancy agreement, Kavin will need to apply for Housing Benefit as soon as possible. We should also check whether he is eligible for Independent Living Fund money to assist his support.

Holiday
Kavin would like a holiday soon, somewhere really warm. He hasn't had one for several years.

Themes
- Kavin wants much more control over his life through the direct payments system. This strong desire brings some consistent conflict with his parents who want (understandably) him to be secure and well cared for. Currently he has a very complicated support system.

- He remembers himself as a competent person with considerable achievements before the injury and now his memory is considerably impaired and mobility very restricted.

- He lives almost entirely in a world peopled by those who have a disability or those who work with them. He wants to live more in the wider world and resume his record of achievements, probably through the Open University.

- The transport seems unnecessarily complex and needs sorting out.

- The next step is to own his own home.

- The various meetings attended by more than a dozen or so professionals involved in Kavin's care indicate a minefield of hidden agendas and concealed philosophies around the desirability or otherwise of increased autonomy for him. Our own fresh involvement complicates matters even further by strengthening (hopefully) the force of his opinion.

Chapter 9
Mary

Kate Atherton

Mary is a frail-looking elderly woman, aged 81 years, with brilliant blue eyes and thin white hair. She is quietly spoken and gentle in manner. She gets respite care in a nursing home on the outskirts of a rural town.

Control
Mary has very little control in her life now. She is cared for ordinarily by her second husband in a ground floor flat in a town some 15 miles away. Currently, her husband is on holiday. Although Mary can walk with a stick she cannot go far without becoming tired. Her meals are prepared by her husband and she needs help with washing and dressing.

Her income is derived from the State pension, attendance allowance, and her industrial pension. Her husband has recently taken out power of attorney. Mary feels that she is being excluded from major decisions in her life and says that she often feels patronised and treated as if she is a two-year-old. She had a major argument with her husband recently (before her entry into respite care) during which she commented: 'I had stuck it for so long and then I flew.' She is very worried now that the relationship with her husband could be over. The prospect of any form of separation from her husband is unthinkable. 'I could not bear it.'

She relies on help to get up and dressed and meals are prepared for her. She goes to bed from 9.30 p.m. onwards and wakes around 6 a.m. She has had incontinence at night although this is alleviated to some extent by her husband who rouses her at least once during the night to use the bedpan. This problem causes a great deal of embarrassment and distress. When incontinence pads were being used, she would remove them neatly during the night, wet the bed, and wake in total confusion.

Skills
Mary's skills have diminished at an alarming speed. Her physical capabilities are restricted as a result of Parkinson's Disease, arthritis, and a heart condition. She can:–
- feed herself if the food is cut up
- walk with the aid of a stick, which she hates, and can climb stairs
- wash herself to some degree although she needs help to reach some areas

take herself to the toilet although she needs help with buttons and zips

read large-print books for short periods of time

watch television

play cards for a limited time

play Scrabble

She likes doing crosswords if someone else writes in the answers, and enjoys listening to music.

She feels very sad that she can do so little now. Until the last two years, she was so active. She played the organ for 50-plus years and sang in several choirs; played bowls; enjoyed travel and holidays, in France in particular; enjoyed gardening and knitting; read widely; attended courses and lectures on a wide range of topics; was a keen photographer; and liked nothing more than taking long walks in the countryside. She also played an active role in different interest groups, acting as secretary to many.

Now she feels low. She acknowledges that her deteriorating health means that not only has she had to give up so much but caused her husband to give up so much in his life too. She senses his resentment and feels powerless. She cannot see any way to improve the situation.

Pain

Throughout her life Mary has suffered from night terrors. She has extremely vivid dreams involving very frightening situations which have resulted in attacks on partners on several occasions. Her confusion (or night terrors) is much worse at night when convinced that she is under attack, from anything from soldiers to a rhinoceros. She has set alarms off fearing intruders and when fully awake could not understand why she had done it.

In her late 50s Mary developed arthritis in her joints and suffered considerable depression as she became convinced that her very active life was over. She then went on to develop an abnormal heart rhythm in which her heart either raced or slowed down to a snail's pace. Either condition resulted in considerable discomfort. A decision was reached by the consultants to try and control the condition by using Digoxin and inserting a pacemaker. Mary was given an early pacemaker in February 1977. This kick-started the heart if it became too slow and drugs were used to try and calm it if it became too fast.

Within two years, her husband of 40 years, to whom she was devoted, had a series of heart attacks and died on Christmas Day 1980. She remarried in May 1982. In 1990, Mary developed a hand tremor and was beginning to have problems with her saliva. The GP referred her to a neurologist who diagnosed Parkinson's Disease. The tremor, gait problem, and dribbling were largely controlled through L-dopa.

The arthritis continued to be a problem until 1991, when walking was extremely difficult and a hip replacement operation recommended. The anaesthetist refused this until a replacement pacemaker was inserted. The two operations took place within a year. By the time the hip operation was scheduled, Mary could hardly walk at all. It was difficult to tell whether the walking difficulties were due to the Parkinsonism or the arthritis.

Mary began to feel depressed but with considerable determination she carried on with her interests. The hip replacement improved her walking considerably. She decided to give up driving, leading to a major loss of independence plus restriction in the kinds of leisure activities that she and her husband both enjoyed.

Gradually her condition has deteriorated still further. She has become increasingly unable to perform day-to-day tasks: a combination of unsteady gait, limited hand control from the tremors, and the arthritis spreading to her shoulder means that she can no longer cut-up food, hold cups without using two hands, play cards, wash herself, or wash up. Even reading the newspaper is a struggle. She has always been short-sighted and now wears bifocal glasses but finds it is difficult to focus for any length of time, her eyes water very easily, and concentration span is very short.

Parkinson's Disease causes severe muscle cramps, sometimes resulting in prolonged periods of complete rigidity. She also becomes increasingly confused at times. Complicated instructions defeat her and she is sometimes confused about time and place. She feels that people patronise her and treat her as a child because she can no longer complete ordinary tasks. She becomes increasingly angry about this. During periods of lucidity, she is fully aware of what is happening. She recognises that she can become extremely depressed and sometimes gets things out of proportion but is very worried about the immediate future. She does not fear death as her strong religious belief suggests that it leads to a far better life. She derives great comfort from regular church attendance.

Contact

Mary lives with her second husband (aged 76) to whom she's absolutely devoted. They have been married for 13 years and lived in a ground floor flat close to the centre of the town in which both had lived for all their working lives.

They had a very active married life, travelling widely, and developing many joint pursuits as well as pursuing their separate interests. They enjoyed a good social life.

Their relationship appears strong although strained. Her husband says that he is surprised to find himself still happy in spite of current difficulties. He admits to finding the situation extremely difficult and sometimes loses his temper with frustration. He still loves Mary and wants to continue to look after her, provided that he can have periods of respite care.

Mary is passionately fond of him and is extremely worried that their relationship will founder. She acknowledges that her various conditions are unlikely to improve and may get worse. She also recognises that not only is her quality of life deteriorating but so is his in having to look after her. She finds his patronising attitude very difficult to handle and fears that having lost her temper once she may do it again, with disastrous consequences. She cannot see a way out as her condition will not go away so that she will continue to become irritated leading to a downward spiral to eventual separation which she could not bear.

Mary has three children from her first marriage all of whom are married and six grown up grandchildren. Her daughters live 60 and 100 miles away respectively and her son eight miles away. Her closest relationships are with her daughters on an emotional level and with her son on a practical level. Since her first husband died contact with all three children is maintained on monthly visits from each. She has shared her current distress with them and hopes that they will help to sort things out. She has very sporadic contact with the grandchildren.

She has a sister who is five years older and who lives six miles away. She lived with Mary's first husband in the family home during the war and left five years after the war ended when Mary's third child was on the way. She is widowed and has no children and is house-bound by choice. Mary and her husband used to visit on a weekly basis until she couldn't manage the bus.

When at home she is visited regularly by neighbours and friends from the church and members of both families. Her husband finds catering very difficult and now that Mary is too self-conscious to eat out such visits tend to be short. Whilst her children are very important, especially at times of stress, in the main her life revolves around her husband and their social life.

Recommendations
1)   Mary wants support to see how serious the problems are between her and her husband. This would involve discussions with them both separately and together.

Mary

2) She needs help to express her frustration and anger about the situation without risking irrevocable marital breakdown

3) Her husband needs individual support to establish his needs and to see how they might be met.

4) Mary needs to look at the possibilities of other activities that she could pursue without feeling patronised. Mary needs help in identifying enjoyable tasks still possible within the limits of her physical capabilities.

5) She needs to be given back much control in her life in terms of money and opportunities to spend it, e.g. taxi fares to see her sister.

6) If Mary's worst fears are realised and her husband feels on return from holiday that he can no longer cope Mary must be given help and support in coping with the consequences.

7) She needs help to further develop the religious connections so significant to her.

Process
First contact
Telephone referral from Mary's husband saying that he had been up half the night with Mary who had been doubly incontinent (diarrhoea) and had spread faeces all over the bedroom. He felt at the end of his tether and could no longer cope. The previous night Mary had set off the alarms in the flat because she thought there was an intruder there. Visit later in the day to establish problem. By the time I arrive the situation is much calmer, her husband is anxious to play down his earlier comments about being at the end of his tether and greets me at the door to tell me that things are all right now and that the bedroom is clean.

Sat with both Mary and her husband to discuss the current situation. At this stage preoccupation is with the continence problem. Mary is extremely distressed at the fuss and cannot understand why it has happened. Looks extremely embarrassed and somewhat uncomfortable. Her husband checked out with her whether she minded talking about it but little real opportunity for her to say no. I explain that I would like to come back to discuss other possible ways of offering help should they like me to.

Practical suggestions made surrounding management of incontinence and referral made to incontinence specialist. Respite care had already been arranged through the GP via contact with The Parkinson's Disease Society

Second contact
A request was made by Mary's husband on behalf of them both for me to return. I invited Mary to tell me her story and the issues as she saw them. Her husband also shared some of his experiences and acknowledged that at times he found coping difficult but reiterated that under no circumstances would he give up. He felt they were very happy, that he loved Mary very much, and wanted to carry on caring. The advice from the incontinence specialist had been very successful and the problem had gone. The medication for Parkinson's Disease was changed to a slow-release pill and that helped enormously.

Third contact
A request was made by the staff at the respite care unit for a visit as Mary seemed agitated and depressed. She was wandering a great deal and was very agitated when asked to come back in.

I visited and found her very quiet and with little prompting she started to tell me very quietly what was troubling her. She started to cry and became very distressed as she explained her dilemmas and worst fears. She'd had no communication from her husband since he'd left for holiday and was desperate to know if she'd 'lost him'. She was very low.

Fourth contact
Phone call from staff: Mary had become extremely agitated and had spilt tea over a care assistant and was hallucinating. She became convinced that the food was poisoned, the room was bugged, and the forces of evil were going to take over. She attacked a staff member with a nail-file, scratching her badly. Doctor prescribed Melleril when required.

Fifth contact
Visited Mary when she had been home for three weeks and she seemed well. Her husband indicated that she wanted to talk to me alone. We spent some time looking at slides of family holidays. Mary told me that she was sitting on a time-bomb. She realised that she had attacked someone and was worried that she would be prosecuted for assault. Although her hallucinations of a large dog – five feet high – had gone, she still saw people standing behind her husband when he came to help. She had caused her husband to lose his balance twice when letting go of his hands to fend off these people. She was very worried that this would be interpreted as a deliberate attempt to harm him. She lives in constant fear of these hallucinations returning.

She was distressed because her husband had bought her a large plastic bib to wear at mealtimes. She had been dropping her food so the washing load had increased considerably. The bib was seen as a way of reducing the amount of laundry. She saw it as humiliating, especially as the fastening was made of Velcro and she couldn't get it off. It was agreed that the bib was destroyed.

She asked for an appointment with her GP to discuss the hallucinations. She was willing to go as a voluntary patient for treatment so the problem could be sorted out. She needed to get away from home as the constant fear and the reactions to her 'odd' behaviour were proving intolerable.

Postscript
Social workers have a tremendous urge to do something and for care plans to have neat and tidy endings. Life is not like that. Mary's story is no exception, as in many situations the carefully prepared care plan could not be put into operation. Her condition worsened and she became violent and aggressive towards her husband, accusing him of stealing and trying to poison her.

Eventually, after much trauma and delay, the GP arranged for her admission to the local psycho-geriatric assessment ward. On arrival Mary announced that she had lost her home, family, friends, and her dignity all for the sake of a few misunderstandings blown up out of all proportion. She said that if this was all there was to life she might just as well walk into the river.

Her condition stabilised for a while as her drug regime was adjusted until she caught a chest infection, when it looked like death was imminent. She rallied again only to hear of plans to admit her to a nursing home and not, as she had thought, to go home. She promptly shut her eyes, refused all food, drink, and medication and died a week later, early in February 1996.

Themes
- Impact of physical and psychological deterioration and eventual death on close relatives.

- Getting the reputation of being 'difficult' in the services. Professionals usually respond defensively.

- Still seeing clients in terms of their strength and potential even though they are unwell and elderly.

- Resisting 'taking over'; trying to ensure that Mary has the power.

Kate Atherton, Althea and David Brandon   'Care Planning Handbook' Positive Publications 1996.

Chapter 10
Debbie

Debbie Tallis

My psychiatric 'career' began in 1991 when I just felt that everything was closing in. I couldn't cope, so took an overdose. Looking back it doesn't seem that an appropriate response, but it was at that time. I've always been predisposed towards depression but it wasn't until Cambridge that it hit me 'big time'! At this stage I had two jobs: I was taking an MSc in London, and started a second job to cover the fees, debt, and travel. I didn't notice for a long time that things weren't right. I was so tired all the time and I couldn't concentrate on taking notes or participate properly in my studies. I managed the first year and went to all the second year lectures but was only there in body – not spirit.

I became physically unwell (may have been more imagined than fact) and ended up in hospital a few times with unstable diabetes. Also around this time, 1990-1, they discovered an underactive thyroid. I was admitted to hospital because of diabetes. I was in a real state as my final MSc exam was the very next day. It was my first encounter with a psychiatrist, who compulsorily sectioned me, even though my instability was justified. I was detained for a few days and discharged. In retrospect, if they had been more supportive and let me do the exam, I'm sure things would not have deteriorated and incarceration within mental hospitals avoided.

However, I started to overdose in September 1991, feeling a failure about not sitting the exams, and desperate and depressed. Overdosing on large amounts of insulin would leave a lump under the skin and take up to four hours before unconsciousness – a long time to reflect. I felt extremely guilty about the hurt I'd cause my parents and friends, even though it would be best for everyone if I was dead. The consequences of causing my own death worried me in religious terms as I was told by some friends how wrong suicide was, and I probably wouldn't go to Heaven. I believed that 'God' would forgive me as 'He' knew what I was feeling – but I worried about where I would go.

I was admitted to a psychiatric hospital on the advice of a psychiatrist who said I needed a hospital stay for proper treatment. He thought I would be in for about three weeks. How wrong he was! I got scared arriving on the ward because the other patients seemed mad and I wasn't, and shouldn't have been there. I considered myself open-minded until that time but my head was filled with stereotypes.

It was very difficult to cope. I couldn't adjust to being a patient. I didn't belong there. I discharged myself after a few days, starting a cycle of going in and out of hospital because I coped neither inside nor outside. I reacted to a combination of hopelessness, helplessness, and desperation by overdosing.

Eventually I was put on a compulsory section because of the 'risk to myself'. I was held against my will in hospital (one being a medium secure unit) for four years. My behaviour was partly due to being out of control and the role reversal of being a patient (used to being a carer). It doesn't justify my actions but explains some behaviour, and rebelling against the system which took away my independence. My friends were exasperated and didn't know what to do, or how, to help. My admission to hospital was some relief as they felt I would be 'looked after and helped'.

During 14 months in a secure hospital, I lived with people responsible for violent crimes. There were two murderers on the ward, and several men had committed sexual offences. I couldn't understand why I deserved a sentence with such people without committing any crime. A fellow inmate tried to strangle me. I was never offered any counselling or support after the attack. Why are women labelled as self-harmers put in such a place? Many women who 'cut up' were sexually abused as children and yet put on a ward with men who have committed such crimes.

I was lucky and got released after 14 months. I had two care plan review meetings, one six months after admission and another four months later. The consultant psychiatrist, consultant clinical psychologist, social worker, psychotherapist, clinical psychologist/psychotherapist, charge nurse, assistant psychologist, and myself all attended. I felt things were going to happen but later found out that because promises are made verbally or written down doesn't make anything happen. The recording was very negative about what I don't do or 'am not willing' to do. I have never seen anything positive in the psychiatric notes. For example, I was taken out one evening and planned to run away. I was very upset and talked to the person who accompanied me (nothing to do with the hospital) and decided I would return. Somehow the hospital discovered, perhaps someone saw me in the taxi, but this was recorded negatively. Everything was about attempts to abscond – not about returning. Nobody was pleased that I hadn't run away. I feel that reactions and punishment – I was not allowed out for some time after – just reinforce flight responses. I had nothing to lose by trying again.

My care plan in June 1995 stated: '. . . has however, not been willing to assess the underlying causes of her depression. If possible she avoids therapies and sessions. . . .' This is untrue and unfair in some respects. I tried all the therapies offered but concluded that they were unsuitable. Playing with a doll or toy car in drama therapy made me wonder who should have been having therapy! At times I did want and need to talk – but there was no one available. It went on, 'Deborah is unlikely to benefit further from treatment'. I didn't get discharged until 14 February 1996.

In September 1995 I had a section 117 meeting to formulate discharge plans. I'd been offered a council flat and paid rent even though I received little money. My social worker, who came with me when I signed for the tenancy, didn't coerce me but without signing I would have lost it. As I had no money I received a small DSS grant for furniture but was not allowed out on my own to look for any. The social worker was always rushed and kept pressing me to get things I didn't want – such as a filthy mattress from a second-hand shop. I couldn't be too choosy but I did want time to look around. I couldn't understand why I was not allowed out on my own. I couldn't go to the flat to sort things out and was only allowed out with someone. It seemed that everyone was always too busy to go to the flat or to help look for equipment. To make matters worse I had a lot of possessions from my previous place which was why I did not want to go into a hostel, as there was never enough space for all my things. This was recorded as unwillingness to accept sheltered accommodation, not the complete story. I did need support from a sheltered place but none had large enough rooms to hold all my belongings, which is why I asked for a flat.

Before taking the tenancy I had a tribunal where I hoped for discharge. It was not to be and I was placed on another compulsory section 3. I built up rent arrears of about £800-900 which I couldn't pay and was very angry that I'd been led along and everything was dashed. I gave up the tenancy as I was unable to leave. Both the housing association and my solicitor were just as angry as I was at the incompetence of the social worker and hospital. I should never have been allowed to take on the flat if they weren't going to allow me to go. All my possessions went back into storage, which my father paid for.

At the subsequent section 117 meeting they discussed

a) 'Due to life-threatening behaviour Debbie should be detained for a long period of further treatment (1-2 years).'

b) Care in this unit increases Debbie's anger and we should explore alternative care or discharge.'

They agreed that 'on balance he (consultant psychiatrist who put me there) inclined towards a move to discharge in the foreseeable future, recognising risks either way. He recommended more elements of a care package should be in place before discharge'. It was not advisable for me to leave hospital until more of the care package was in place, and that my wish to go and sort things out after discharge was viewed as too risky. I met the criteria for the At Risk Register – 'a significant risk of self-harm' but this needed endorsement by the relevant medical officer.

The second and last care plan review meeting in October 1995 again stated my unwillingness to participate in therapies and that hospitalisation would not benefit my mental state. They listed immediate objectives but I don't recall elements like 'improve self-image' by 'addressing diet and improve functioning in social situations' which are noted on the record. I needed help in gaining confidence, in trying to be intelligent by doing something educational where I could think and converse.

My final 117 meeting in December 1995 discussed the tribunal not discharging me and recommended a further opinion be sought about the appropriateness of further detention and whether I be treated at the unit or elsewhere. 'It was recognised that Deborah will require more than out-patient and day care. Another worker, either a community psychiatric nurse, occupational therapist, or social worker can be made available from the locality team. The Project (Turning Point) would be additional support.'

I had another tribunal on the 8 January 1996 and was given a conditional discharge to sort out somewhere to live. I was really pleased that I'd nearly served my 'sentence', but all I wanted to do was to get out to kill myself. Part of me wanted to live but there were so many barriers ahead. I went to stay with my parents on the 9 February for the weekend as I still had no keys to a flat I was offered until the 19th. My father took me to see the flat before we went to Kent that weekend. It was absolutely filthy, with nothing on the floors and awful colours underneath all the dirt. I was really upset and planned to take an overdose when returning to the hospital on the Monday. I stored insulin and hid it for the big day.

Looking back I realise how nasty it was to plan suicide as I was so hurt and angry at the hospital for detaining me for such a long time. Everything went wrong that night. I had carefully planned my demise and would cause a 'stink' in that difficult questions would get asked. I wanted the hospital investigated because it wasn't a 'therapeutic environment' at all. It was containment, where inmates were often treated like animals.

I managed to take a very large dose of insulin before going to sleep. I believed that when staff 'looked in' they would just think I was asleep. However, through stupidity, I asked to speak to a nurse, as I wanted to 'say good-bye', thank her (some staff were OK at times), and tell her that I was leaving the next day. She took over an hour to see me. I'd injected insulin so many times, it would take many hours before unconsciousness. Unfortunately it affected me quicker than I thought. She came to see me and I just said good-bye and thank you. She asked if I was all right. I said that my blood sugar might be a bit low. I don't remember much about that evening, except awaking in the general hospital the next day feeling very ill.

I discharged myself two days later from both the general hospital and the psychiatric one, as at that stage I was 'informal'. I was offered no help to get my possessions to Cambridge or move into my flat. They hadn't even bothered to find out if I had the tenancy, which I did not. I went straight to my GP to get a prescription to kill myself again. I felt so depressed and desolate. I was glad to leave but very scared at being on my own after such a long time. I felt at a loss and everything seemed futile.

I didn't see the social worker until five weeks after discharge even though at all my 117 meetings and care plans it was stated that I needed much support. I got help from the Gwydir Project who were extremely helpful in many ways. They realised that the flat was not habitable and organised some young people doing community service to clean and paint it. They supported me emotionally and practically in piecing things together.

Eventually I had a care plan meeting which my father attended. I was not offered anything helpful. I needed to talk to someone and had to fight to see a CPN. After all the discussions in the meetings, it was just a word game to these professionals. So long as they were seen trying to do things then their backs were covered if anything happened. They weren't working in my best interests. I am not the easiest person to help or get on with in hospital. It must have been very frustrating and exasperating for staff. Not all staff or services were bad and I like and respect some individuals but feel that they cannot really say what they feel as they are part of the system.

The health authority spent well over a quarter of a million pounds on my supposed care. I feel quite angry about this, as all along psychiatrists and health care professionals said that hospital did not help me. So why was I in for so long? Why didn't they just let me get on with it? That's what I have done since leaving. I didn't even know whether I would survive, but I have! I did and do need help, but when asking for help like counselling I'm denied this and told that I'm 'untreatable'. How do they know? I am untreatable in a hospital but not now.

If you're able to ask for help, psychiatrists think you are well enough to cope, even though you may say you can't or you feel suicidal. I feel the only way to get help is overdosing, not to kill myself but to get help. I've been told 'not to be so silly'. But it's not silly. It is asking for help before getting to the point when you can't go on, diffusing the crisis. I've met many people in my 'psychiatric career', several are now dead. When asking for help some have been turned away. It's too late when dead to get help.

I should have been helped in the community. At times I needed someone all the time – cheaper than what happened. I needed help to gain confidence and self-worth, to be encouraged when well enough to do some work and reading. Not being brushed aside and dismissed as a non-person and labelled 'a manipulative attention seeker'. It's not true but even if I was, shouldn't professionals find out why? I've only ever tried to kill myself when very depressed. It's been said that I am unwilling to look at the underlying causes of my depression. I believe it is organic in origin. When I get depressed it's not because something triggers it off. If things are not working it doesn't help, but it's not causal. I needed help in hospital to learn to cope differently when feeling suicidal. Nobody ever addressed this problem.

I do resent the time spent in hospital against my will which was 'for my own good'. If I could have trusted and talked about my feelings, maybe things would not have got so out of hand. I was locked up and isolated as if I were a criminal and the only things gained when in hospital were less self-confidence, self-esteem, and self-worth, and physically two sizes!

A better alternative with all that money spent would have been a period at a health farm and a relaxing holiday. It would have been cheaper and much more therapeutically effective!

I am assertive enough now to ask for what I need (of course this is seen as manipulative!). I did stop seeing mental health professionals for about six months as I felt very let down. They would say one thing but write something completely different in the notes. I have started to see my social worker again, who has been supportive and helpful, and also visit a cognitive behavioural therapist, but it has taken a long, hard battle.

I am actually getting there but it wouldn't have been possible without the support and love from friends and family. I am very lucky but there are many who aren't. Many can't say what they need, or can be so forceful; to get appropriate help shouldn't be as hard. I thank those who 'hung in with me' throughout those awful years as well as since. I've met many people in voluntary organisations and elsewhere who've been both helpful and supportive. It has been users and ex-users of mental health services as well as other organisations which have kept me going, along with those close to me.

Themes
- Debbie didn't feel listened or responded to. The nature of her immense distress was not recognised.
- She found herself on a psychiatric juggernaut which spent hundreds of thousands of pounds in detaining her. This was not a service designed for a unique need. She lost even more confidence and gained a fresh and thoroughly undesirable career. One result was that she was attacked by a fellow patient and received no support – inherent dangers in mixed sex psychiatric units.
- Meetings which led to decisions, very rarely implemented. For example, her care programme for discharge was never put into action. She moved from an intensely support-secure setting in the community and was neglected in that dangerous initial transition period (high suicide rate).
- Labelled as a 'borderline personality disorder' she found this extremely destructive.
- She didn't feel any sort of partnership with the various hospital staff. She was just seen as a manipulative nuisance.
- Practical problems like the tenancy of the flat and social security were handled badly.
- Robust struggle to gain relevant support in the community. It's not clear if she ever had a keyworker.

Chapter 11
My Daughter Clare

Jan Thurlow

There cannot be many caring parents who have not at times stood back and wondered what the future holds for their children, particularly as they grow through teenage years into the adult world. I know I have. I was particularly concerned about my daughter Clare, when she was on the brink of adulthood and about to leave full-time education. I wondered what she would do in her life, where she would live, if she would have good friends, be respected and treated for the energetic, resilient, yet sensitive, person she is. Would her greed for life be appreciated as well as her sense of humour, and her affectionate, loving qualities that she freely gives? Would her abilities to forgive and lift your sometimes-dampened spirits with her hearty laughter and a hug as well as her ability to keep a confidence as faithfully as any good counsellor, be acknowledged? I was concerned, and still am, that those around her should really like her, treat her with the dignity and give her the respect I think she deserves. Would they look out for her, share in her joys and console her in her sad or frustrated moments; but most of all would they accept her as the person she is, and still be there for her? For Clare was born with Down's syndrome, and has other hidden disabilities that leave her highly dependent on able people around her to live all aspects of her life.

Clare spent 17 years in the segregated education system, attending the same 'special' school; staying virtually in the same class of pupils, none of whom could speak, all highly dependent on able people around them, all of whom did not really relate to one another but instead preferred the attention of, and interaction with, the able members of staff and helpers in the class. As a result of this experience, I felt it was crucial that the first steps into adulthood after leaving school were well worked out, to enable Clare to develop and flourish in this new phase of her life. Indeed, the last few years spent in school were, I suspect, not unlike those of many other teenagers: they had lost their lustre. In Clare's case this became very evident through her expressions of frustration in her behaviour and communication, as well as her frequent reluctance to leave the car that had taken her there. If that wasn't saying 'I don't really want to be here' I don't know what was.

Over the years it became very evident that super-high-class services were not handed out on a plate; indeed, in my experience, there were no such services anyway. The respite supports, such as they were, had to be fought for against the backdrop of the familiar statements about funding cuts; the withdrawal of the scant, less than ideal service, which was all that was offered, drove me to leaving my very vulnerable child in a long-stay hospital for respite care, an horrendously painful experience and one I would never wish to repeat; imagining what is was like for Clare made it hurt even more.

As a result of Clare's past very poor experiences within the statutory sector, I have found myself over the years swimming against the tide of the service system. Indeed, the services she had received taught me well and eroded my trust. It didn't take me long to realise that, so very often, it is people with learning disabilities who enter into human support systems as people and are immediately turned into 'clients' and are processed and treated as such. In the conversion they have very little say or control over their lives, have few friendships and meaningful relationships, are often very lonely, are amongst the poorest in society, and open to abuse.

When Clare was in her mid-teens I realised that the plans for her life after leaving school must not be left too late. As Clare had already been physically and mentally abused in a small community 'unit' run by the health authority, my husband and 1 were adamant that Clare was not going into further institutionally run services after leaving school – enough was enough. We also knew that the picture was not rosy and choices were very limited, if indeed there were any. I had a hunch that Clare would have been considered too disabled to attend the local adult training centre, and that a high needs day care centre would have been the option on offer, we didn't have either of those places in mind for Clare anyway. No! We wanted Clare to experience everyday life; she didn't need fixing, changing, or training, – she just needed to be able to develop the skills she had and be who she was.

Some years ago I had the opportunity to travel to Vancouver, and learn from the parents there who had pioneered service brokerage and individualised funding. I decided to take a leaf from their book and set up a circle of support around Clare, particularly as we do not have the Canadian-style service brokerage and individualised funding in place, or the advantage of an independent agent/broker to work alongside Clare. The circle consisted of a few people who had known Clare over the years; we met, together with Clare, regularly around my kitchen table and began by looking to the future, to imagine what dreams and hopes there were. We pooled our ideas and thoughts, bearing in mind Clare's likes and dislikes, her personality and her strengths, looked at the things she liked to do, and shared ideas about what she may like to do but had never had the opportunity to try. Armed with our understanding and knowledge of Clare we all came to the same conclusion – that Clare needed able people around her to support her, people who could really get to know her, and with time help her develop, and who would become expert in Clare's way of communicating. It seemed reasonable to think that the funding that would have been spent on a placement at the day care centre could instead fund people for Clare.

A few months before Clare left school, she had a formal assessment carried out by the social worker responsible for school-leavers, who also had attended some of the circle meetings. Looking back, the circle must have been quite an intimidating experience for her, but at the same time it gave us an opportunity to explain what we had in mind for Clare. What had always concerned me was that a formal statutory assessment was being carried out on my daughter by a social worker who had very little knowledge or insight into Clare; meeting Clare a few times in the classroom did not give a true picture. Like all of us, it takes time to get to know people, and I shuddered at the thought of any future day-time plan being made from the scant knowledge that could be gleaned from a few meetings. We couldn't bear the thought of Clare being offered a service in another institution, which, had it been left to the formal assessment, would have been the case.

It was crazy was that, when the contracts had been drawn up between the voluntary agency looking after Clare and the health authority, there were no future plans worked out for the funding of Clare when she left school. Whether it was thought she was going to evaporate into thin air, or whether it was automatically assumed that social services would pick up the bill, I don't know. If the situation hadn't been so worrying it was almost laughable.

However, there is an adage 'a blessing in disguise'. I cannot truly say that Clare being placed in a long-stay hospital, albeit initially for respite, or her being abused in the health authority 'community units', was a blessing – far from it. But what was a blessing, if a rather mixed one, was that Clare had always been funded by the health authority in all of her residential placements. Prior to Clare leaving school she was, and still is, living in a three-bedded group home, run by a voluntary organisation and funded by the health authority. As a result of this, the authority did agree to commit funding for Clare, which is where our challenge lay. Even though the assessment for day services had been carried out by the social worker, we had to look to the health authority to fund the plan. I, along with the circle of support, had put in a lot of time and energy puffing the plan together and costing it out on a needs-led basis. Accompanied by Clare's new social worker responsible for adult services (as Clare was now 19) I visited the funding negotiators of the health authority. It didn't seem to matter that we had a carefully-worked-out, person-centred, needs-led plan of her day supports. We could have saved ourselves a lot of bother in the first place and just asked what they were prepared to give us as they appeared to have already made up their minds. Sadly, we succeeded in getting just over half the amount of money we asked for. I didn't know whether to laugh or cry. Laugh, because something is better than nothing; or cry, because we would be really struggling to meet the needs that Clare had, to give her a reasonable chance in living a life properly supported, not just existing.

All that happened just over a year ago. Clare, to her relief, left school in July 1996. Her personal supporters had been appointed and started working alongside her within a week of her leaving school. On the whole, things have gone very well, though there have been a few 'blips'. Some supporters have come and gone, which is something I have learnt to become immune to over the years, and some have stayed. But I am still here with my family, and the circle of support is still around, though we have not met as regularly. But soon we will be meeting again around my kitchen table, pooling our thoughts and energies into puffing stage two into action, once the funding is finally released. This will be for a home of Clare's own, through a do-it-yourself ownership scheme; and increasing the number of personal assistants around Clare, to enable her to enjoy all aspects of her daily life.

Yet it seems there is 'no gain without pain'. The inordinate amount of time taken by the health authority to undo the block funding that presently covers Clare in her group home is time out of Clare's life. She lives in a situation you or I would not tolerate, from which she is helpless to escape unless we fight beside her and for her. There are times when the situation becomes so exasperating, and one's spirit becomes so low, that one wonders where the next ounce of energy is going to come from to fight on. Yet being with Clare, seeing her smile, hearing her hearty laughter, receiving her unconditional love and her hugs, to me make the battle worth while.

Themes
- Dealing with the abuse of a disabled daughter by the services which are supposed to care for her.
- Specific problems of someone profoundly disabled and unable to express their needs verbally and protest about abuse.
- Seeking fresh ways of organising services so that she and her daughter can have much more autonomy.
- Developing a 'circle of support'.

Chapter 12
Visions?

If there is a modern-day equivalent of helpers passing by on the road to Jericho, it is in mental health. The juxtaposition of mental illness and community care is the basis of much social confusion and fear. How many passers-by are in Monica's story?

She is 28 years old, 5ft 2ins and four stones overweight. This would normally be enough to attract negative attention but she also stands in the street tearing at her clothes and yelling at people driving or walking past. *'Lord Jesus save us from evil... we're enslaved... let your people go'.* Given the number of people that rush past, it seems the exodus has already started. The people who know her pass by at a considerable distance and wonder where her mother is. Those who don't know only see a potential axe murderer and cursing community care under their breath as they hurry past, training seriously for the Olympics.

Gavin is the weary duty worker at the local SSD. He gets a call from her sister. *'My mother is with me and she's had enough of my sister. She can't stand it any more. She shouldn't have to put up with it.'* Monica has said several times that she wants to move but no one took any notice because they see it as a feature of her particular learning disability.

Gavin types the lengthy details into the office computer. He learns that the team has no responsibility for Monica because her learning disability is combined with the mental illness. He breathes a sigh of relief and passes the enquiry on to the mental health team. The duty worker says Monica is not their pigeon either and suggests Gavin try the specialist learning disability team. Monica's dual diagnosis means a sophisticated argument, like a version of musical chairs with both teams wanting to lose. *Meanwhile the woman by the wayside is unconscious!*

The next duty worker takes down the details on a special form and discusses the situation with her line manager, who suggests further investigation. A care manager named Mary is allocated and visits the home. Mary is a devoted Roman Catholic, early mass each day. She was called to a career in welfare work – a religious vocation, with a strong desire to be of service to others. Fifty years ago she'd have been a convent Mother Superior. Mary believes devoutly in the second coming of Christ and is sympathetic to Monica's outbursts. She keeps these thoughts silent in case her own mental health is questioned. Over identifying with the clients is bad form.

Monica's mother learnt from a friend that she must reject her daughter to make her eligible for services. She is learning to play the complicated system. *'I know this isn't easy but if they think you're willing to carry on they'll do nothing'* her friend instructs. Taking this advice, because her friend is an insider, the mother tells Mary, tearfully, that she can't cope any more and no longer accepts any responsibility for Monica.

Mary will try to arrange crisis accommodation for Monica. She also calls Monica's GP who is on sick leave and the locum is out on calls. She contacts the local health team. They say that Monica is unknown to them and it *'sounds like a social care issue anyway'* but if she'd like to make a referral they'd discuss it at the next allocation meeting but *'. . . we can't promise anything because we're all rushed off our feet'*. Everyone is so busy and drowning in paperwork.

Monica's sister sits with her while the care manager contacts local short-term care agencies. There is a shortage of beds in the area and she rings around trying to find one. There should be an emergency bed but this has already been taken by a disturbed homeless woman earlier that day. There's no room at the various inns.

Her sister can't have Monica at her house because she's no room but says that if there's a problem in finding a bed there's this couple in the next village who might look after her for a week or two. They'd only ask for expenses and they already know Monica and the whole family. The care manager explains wearily that this option is impossible, even though it's cheaper and with people they know, because the couple are not a recognised agency. *'They have to be registered by the local authority.'*

Short-term care for another person with disabilities is cancelled to accommodate, by this time, the bad-tempered Monica. There are no vacancies in any other local group homes so this arrangement may run to several weeks. This particular home only supports people between the hours of 4 p.m. and 10 a.m. – from tea-time to breakfast.

The care manager still has to arrange support for the hours in between, as well as for the transport. The most expedient option is to ferry Monica to a day centre. The centre want to know a lot more before accepting the referral. The manager asks: *'Is she violent? Can we have a risk assessment on the appropriate forms?'* Yet another phone call, several more long forms are completed. In total, getting Monica a bed took 12 phone calls, five meetings, and six forms, a partridge in a pear-tree – and this is still only temporary respite!

What happens if we analyse these various structural blocks? We can use the four magnets to help.

Control

> *'The truth is this: we do need you, not to be 'experts' or managers of our lives, but to be friends, enablers and receivers of our 'gifts' to you. We need you to admit cheerfully what you don't know, without shame; to ask us what we need before providing it, to lend us your physical strength when appropriate, to allow us to teach you necessary skills; to champion our rights, to remove barriers previously set in place, to return to us any power you may have had over our lives. We may also need you to remind us of our importance to the world, and to each other, at times of tiredness and discouragement. We can live without patronage, pity and sentimentality, but we cannot live without closeness, respect and co-operation from other people. Above all we need you to accept any 'segregation' of one group of humans from another as anything else but an unacceptable loss for all concerned.'* (Mason and Rieser 1990)

There are some fairly obvious power imbalances between workers and service users in deciding what gets on the agenda, whose needs are recognised or ignored, what the eligibility criteria are, even what form the alternatives to traditional services can take. . . . Most major decisions are already made long before any clients and relatives even appear on the scene. The service is shaped largely by professionals. The long chain of command extends all the way up through local to central government but we all too often blame government and deny personal responsibility. *'They wouldn't let us do this . . .'* when we didn't even ask. Often nobody can be found to take any responsibility. *'My hands were tied. It was more than my job was worth.'*

Care planning can become a bureaucratic steeplechase with its own mystifying language/jargon. This particular language is essentially exclusive, rarely understood by service users or their relatives. Front-line workers are also deprofessionalised and deskilled with less opportunity to use any training and education. They are simply clerks with less and less discretion and control as organisations move increasingly towards standardisation, uniformity, and centralisation.

Care managers are supposed to co-ordinate the efforts of a team of different professionals. Multidisciplinary working can mean an expensive nightmare. We have uncovered in our care plan for Judy, a multiply disabled young woman living in Northumberland, involvement by more than 50 professionals, many hardly on speaking terms with each other. Meetings were a confused mess. All the participants seem to have widely varying agendas and no agreement on general goals. (Brandon 1994) This was a recipe for considerable conflict, which included two advisers who rowed continually and a special school headmistress who wouldn't let me or anybody else in to see how Judith was progressing.

One of the Herculean tasks of care management is to bring this kind of warfare towards some reconciliation. (Wolk *et al*.1994) Staff, carers, and other stakeholders have got to believe and centre on the autonomy of the service user. We saw how really difficult that could be in Joan's chapter, with more evidence of the paternalism of some residential establishments. Her individual needs clash with the block treatment of the old people's home. It is sinful to bother anybody in authority so she can largely be ignored. She is fitted firmly into a regimented system. *'The care plan ought not to be published because it would upset the staff.'* The system is carefully protected against user feedback. Users who complain are simply troublemakers. Blame the victim!

The less control staff have, the more stress they tend to experience. More provision is run by private companies with the corresponding scaling down of state provision. Continuous and secure employment is less available. Voluntary bodies and charities also become entangled in these tentacles. The power of funding is all-invasive. The voluntary sector in the UK is in danger from the 'paradigm of conflict' (Kendall and Knapp 1997). The fiscal power of the national lottery also has a major impact.

Of course there are service users who want to relinquish control. They don't want to know about alternative services, self-help initiatives, or even what their medication is for. They want professionals or relatives to accept responsibility. These are extremely complicated processes. The decision to give up control or collude is not easy. As with Winston in Orwell's '1984', clients and relatives can find it easier to accept the Party's truth inside their own heads. For still others, surrendering control helps them to feel safer. They have become service addicts used to seeing the specialists, touching the feudal forelock, pursuing the 'magic bullet', needing management guidelines to govern their behaviour. Services can both resent and enjoy the dependency of these 'junkies'. There are some very strong sado-masochistic undertones.

Debbie's chapter caught many of these dilemmas. Her frequent overdoses were a pressing plea for professionals to take some responsibility for her life. Once inside the services, she felt not listened to, part of a service juggernaut just rolling on like 'Old Man River . . .'. Nothing seemed designed for her specific needs. That psychiatric juggernaut was immensely expensive and probably ineffective.

When she wanted to take more responsibility she wasn't allowed to, or given mixed messages. She was encouraged to find and rent a flat by the social worker and then the authorities opposed her discharge at the mental health review tribunal. At one moment, apparently, she needs intensive care and treatment and, at the next, discharged into the community; she has to fight fiercely for rudimentary support in an unprepared flat at the time of the highest suicidal risk.

Kirsty's social worker helped her to gain autonomy. 'She was fantastically dynamic and organised, able not only to listen but also to hear.' She steered away from the negatives and negotiated with the relevant agencies to facilitate the service user's wishes. She understood that her role was mainly to enable.

There are no good reasons why people with disabilities cannot take a much greater role in care management and professional training. CCETSW offers guidance in the involvement of users in social work training. (Beresford 1994) Leader offers specific help on care planning for psychiatric survivors, cutting out the professional middle person. (Leader 1995) It means the transferring of power to users.

A genuine transfer of power is possible. In a study of mental health service users and the care programme approach, Carpenter showed that nearly all the sample had found it 'sufficiently clear and addressing their needs adequately'. Users responded positively and, compared with those outside the system, were better informed about rights and services. Two remaining deficiencies were an ignorance about the side-effects of medication, and complaints procedures. (Carpenter 1996)

Skills
Joan felt very fearful of losing her key skills. Due to her right-sided weakness, she could no longer hold a book to read and failing sight made that even more problematic. She fears even further deterioration. The lack of provision of adequate numbers of large-print books unnecessarily increases her difficulties. Her impairment combined with service deficiencies involves increased distress. The services should assist in maintaining skills and even developing fresh ones.

Effective care planning depends on professional skills, on the capacity of professionals to listen effectively as well as to advocate. Real listening is extremely difficult. Structural factors such as huge case-loads and draconian management systems have their adverse impact. It can be hard to focus on one person when your mind is buzzing with the list of priorities for just one day.

Sinason points out the extent to which staff are rendered stupid. (Sinason 1992) They are unable to cope with the large burden of grief experienced in daily contact with their clients. They have little support, supervision, or relevant training. Staff sickness rates are extremely high. Many are numbed by massive bureaucracy. Care managers feel deskilled and increasingly have less power.

There is a powerful argument for devolving budgets further down in organisations which might relieve some of the tensions between power and responsibility felt by the practitioners, but the main political pressures are towards centralisation. Cornwell had wisely predicted that 'the pressure on resources is likely to intensify the dynamic of reliance on professional assessments to legitimate bureaucratic decisions, creating a process which facilitates the emergence of a class of professional bureaucrats'. (Cornwell 1992)

Advocacy is a core skill. There is little point in listening, however expertly, if the case for the client's needs is not well made to the providing organisation. Listening to Max (Chapter 4) was followed up by skilful presentation and innovative negotiation. This advocacy role is often in conflict with the gatekeeping, inherent in the assessment stage.

'Many case managers have two roles, that of gatekeeper and that of advocate, that often conflict. A true advocate adopts the client's perspective as the guide for activity. Many advocacy models exist, notably those of physician/patient and lawyer/client. The client's rights to an informed choice and to strict confidentiality are fundamental to these advocacy models and must be incorporated into any advocacy model of case management.' (Dubler 1992) Allowing that the author has obviously never tried to instruct a solicitor or to tell a family doctor what is wrong, advocacy is a core skill!

The sheer scale of change taking place as experienced by many professionals makes the practice increasingly fraught and difficult . . .

> 'I knew my work had changed for ever when I found the shiny new calculator on my desk.'
>
> 'If I had wanted to be an accountant I wouldn't have bothered doing the Diploma in Social Work.'
>
> 'I have to do masses of admin. I've just photocopied 30 forms. Is this really what the state is paying me to do? I must be the highest paid photocopier in the country!'
>
> 'The structure demands flexibility and compliance. Like Alice in Wonderland we drink the potion and are malleable.'
>
> 'I had such hopes for care management as a vehicle for change. I was naïve.'
>
> 'If I didn't have a mortgage to pay I'd be out.'
>
> 'The forms are okay if you just think of them as a guide.'
>
> 'Expectations are high yet resources, financial and personal, are low.'

We can also learn from the volunteers. After all the word 'amateur' comes from the Latin verb 'to love'. Collective forms of advocacy can surmount obstacles, e.g. to open up even the social security labyrinths. Community development and action, e.g. credit unions and other self-help schemes, are also invaluable.

People need the skills to start groups like People First. Gary Bourlet, along with eight others with disabilities, began People First in the UK in 1984. Bourlet has a vision for a continental European organisation, hoping that people with learning difficulties in continental Europe as well as in the UK would receive training. *'We don't want to be set up to fail. There is a need for training, for self-advocates to train others'.* (Bourlet 1995)

The development of direct payments, legitimised by the Direct Payments (Social Services) Act 1996, with the relevant professional skills can help. Kirsty and Kavin are both struggling along that route and will need a variety of supports from professionals. They need trained people with a sound values base who respect their capacity to survive and achieve. (Holman and Collins 1997)

Pain

People's expectations of community care are high and the existing funding can't deliver. There is a wide gap between the pain and distress felt by many individuals and what they want and need from the various services. The government's (of whatever colour) response is to abandon fundamental parts of the Welfare State.

'We can't afford it' is the prevalent mantra. In a wealthy country like ours, we can afford it if we choose to. The real question is whether we should. It's a huge question about social equality and inclusion which involves moral and economic issues. Collective responsibility is what makes us social beings.

We can see how the residential service increases the pain and isolation felt by Joan. She's afraid of losing control, of being increasingly dependent, and the nature of the service increases her loneliness and separation. What staff provide is not on the top of her agenda, which is not about hygiene and cleanliness but warmth and contact. To narrow the great gap between service intent and the outcomes for users is extremely difficult.

Jan felt really powerless when her daughter with Down's syndrome was misused and abused by institutional staff. She couldn't get much needed information about what was going on and the stress and guilt were immense. One day she even found her daughter dressed in someone else's clothes. Staff seemed to lack empathy and any direction.

Anya Souza writes of her lifelong battle against the label 'Downs syndrome'. 'It takes a lot of courage to fight against people who have the power to define who you are. People who think they can define you also assume they can tell you what your rights are and, because of who they think you are, specify what you should do with your life.' (Ramcharan *et al.* 1997 p4)

We saw how Monica gets completely lost in the process of care management. Her pain and distress and needs get overwhelmed and forgotten in an immensely complicated bureaucratic process which can allow for little flexibility. *Agency Requirements United 6: Monica 0.* She became an object simply manipulated and processed in whatever way the services chose.

'Don't you realise that I can feel
Your need to change him
Your need for him to be other than as he is
To be 'improved'
To be more or less or whatever
You are disturbed by?

Don't you understand that
The comments you make about my child
Tell about yourself
And not about him?'
(Murray and Penman 1996 p4)

Staff get pained and demoralised by huge, complex, bureaucratic processes. 'The number of forms has mushroomed and the weight of administrative procedures seems to be correlated with the extent to which the purchaser/provider split has developed.' (Lewis *et al.* 1997)

Parents and in particular mothers are still pawns in the community care game and their pain often goes unrecognised. Caring is hard work and has low status. There is an expectation that mothers will continue to care for their children way beyond childhood. We take this work for granted and collude with it being unpaid because we believe that payment brings the cash factor into love. A poor, patriarchal argument as we approach the twenty-first century.

Contact
This is a vital part of the process because of both the nature of relationships between worker and user and the wider community contact. We can see that Joan, for example, is losing more and more contact with the world outside the home. She is part of this grossly segregated world we have carefully constructed. The staff don't have the time or perhaps even the vision to see how important those connections are. Their work is centred upon cleaning and providing practical services. They don't see making relationships as important, even though, in their own daily lives, fun and friendship are probably vital.

Poverty prevents people from getting out and joining in. You need money to drink in a pub or eat in a restaurant or to take a bus or taxi. Most of our chapters describe the struggle with lack of money. Max and his mother struggle to remain in the valued world through the constant struggle with poverty. It is easy for them to get forced into a financial ghetto, to get into more and more debt. Their rent arrears nearly stopped them from moving to somewhere much more suitable and amenable.

Some finance is essential for mixing. Currently there is almost a denial of poverty with sparse research. If we are going to help people mix more then we must have evidence of the impact of poverty. Accessibility is also crucial – there is not much point in going to the pub if you can't get your wheelchair through the door. There are also many obstacles to obtaining paid work yet employment is a major way in which people can be part of their community. There are still many apartheid systems which effectively cut people off – special schools, care villages, day centres. The structure also finds sexuality, especially gay and lesbian orientations, hard to cope with.

Effective contact is also complicated because we seem imprisoned in the entirely separate roles of professionals and clients. The welfare system is based on differentiation between "us" and "them" with no stress on commonalities. Many care planners have experience of the services, either as clients or relatives. They are the sons and daughters of elderly people in residential care or the parents of children with learning difficulties.

Expectations of community care simply increase with each generation. Joan's 'daughters' won't be so passive when they get old. They have learnt to demand more and expect higher standards. They have an identity as consumers in supermarkets or travel agents,but not as possessors of ideas of rights – which has a knock-on effect for health and social services. They know how to complain and access support. They will make more trouble for staff.

In care planning, there are always considerable traps in the contact area. An over-protective approach emphasises safety and leads to a mountain of risk-assessment procedures and demolishing half an Amazonian forest. It can result in smothering people so they are unable to live meaningful lives. It can often mean a form of institutionalised living within the community. It erodes autonomy.

For example, Joe was refused permission to go fishing, which he loves, because of the danger of being 'close to the water so he might fall in'. Difficult to fish without being close to water! A professional colleague goes out socially with a woman with learning difficulties. She received a longish letter from the social services department asking about her intentions and purposes in this relationship. '... who is going to supervise the pub visits, the horse riding ...' That way lies complete madness.

People demand forms of professional safety and security which are unrealistic. If the balloon goes up, they don't want any responsibility. Risk assessments become structural justification for this arrant nonsense going far beyond what can be seen as reasonable care. Such assessments, requests for which are becoming more common, are simply about the 'covering of backs'. 'It wasn't my responsibility. I filled in the necessary forms, asked the relevant people for permission. . . .'

As with over-protection, detachment is based on a fundamental misunderstanding of professionalism. Users have felt staff were always looking at them through a plate glass window – distant and largely uninvolved. There was no sharing and very little human warmth. Detachment protects the professional, seeing others as observed objects. It can be the worst feature of poor assessment work with the service user, the real expert on their needs, simply getting further excluded.

> 'There's a light inside Kim – it's like a warm candle glowing. It's all orangey. Sometimes the candle gets blown out and the warmth stops, but if you pay a bit of attention to him it comes back. Sometimes the light goes out when he is poorly, sometimes the light goes out when he is excluded. It glows most brightly when he is well and when he is at the centre of things.'
> (Jessie Murray – his sister in Murray and Penman p93)

References

Beresford P. *Changing the Culture – involving service users in social work education* CCETSW 1994

Bourlet G. *People First in Europe* Conference Report 1995 Hampshire Coalition of Disabled People

Brandon D. and A. *Yin and Yang of Care Planning* Anglia Polytechnic University 1994

Carpenter J. and Sbaraini S. 'Involving service users and carers in the Care Programme Approach' *Journal of Mental Health*, vol 5, no 5 (pp483-8) 1996

Cornwell N. 'Assessment and Accountability in Community Care' *Critical Social Policy* 1992

Dubler N.D. 'Individual Advocacy as a Governing Principle' *Journal of Case Management,* vol 1, no 3, Autumn 1992 (pp82-6)

Holman A. and Collins J. *Funding Freedom – direct payments for people with learning difficulties* Values into Action, 1997

Hutton W. *The State to Come* Vintage 1997

Kendall J. and Knapp M. quoted in Welfare and Values, *Challenging the Culture of Unconcern* edited by Askonas P. and Frowen S.F. Macmillan 1997

Leader A. *Direct Power: a resource pack for people who want to develop their own care plans and support networks* MIND/Pavilion 1995

Lewis J. *et al.* 'Implementing Care Management: Issues in relation to the new Community Care' *British Journal of Social Work*, 1997, vol 27 (pp 5-24)

Mason M. and Rieser R. *Disability Equality in the Classroom: a human rights issue* ILEA 1990

Murray P. and Penman J. (compilers) *Let our Children be – a collection of stories* Parents with Attitude 1996

Orwell G. *Nineteen Eighty-Four*

Ramcharan P. *et al.* (Editor) *Empowerment in Everyday Life – Learning Disability* Jessica Kingsley 1997

Sinason V. *Mental Handicap – the human condition* Free Association 1992

Wolk J. L. *et al.* 'The Managerial Nature of Case Management' *Social Work* (USA) 39 (2) March 1994